2/01

The Collected Earlier Poems

By William Carlos Williams (in print)

In the American Grain (prose)
Selected Poems
A Dream of Love (a play)
Make Light of It (collected stories)
Paterson (a poem)
In the Money (a novel)
The Collected Later Poems
The Collected Earlier Poems

The Collected Earlier Poems of

WILLIAM
CARLOS
WILLIAMS

A NEW DIRECTIONS BOOK

Contents

The Wanderer   1

The Tempers   13

March · History   41

History   47

Della Primavera Trasportata Al Morale   55

An Early Martyr   83

Al Que Quiere (To Him Who Wants It)   115

Fish · Romance Moderne   175

Sour Grapes   185

Paterson · The Flower   231

Spring and All   239

Struggle of Wings   289

The Descent of Winter   295

Impromptu: The Suckers   313

Collected Poems 1934   319

An Elegy for D. H. Lawrence   359

Adam and Eve and the City   365

Morning · The Crimson Cyclamen   391

Recent Verse 1938   405

The Drunkard   435

INDEX OF POEMS BY TITLES   467

Acknowledgments

The poems from *An Early Martyr* and *Adam & Eve & The City* are included through the courtesy of Ronald Land Latimer of the Alcestis Press, who first published them in limited editions.

The Wanderer

The Wanderer

A ROCOCO STUDY

ADVENT

Even in the time when as yet
I had no certain knowledge of her
She sprang from the nest, a young crow,
Whose first flight circled the forest.
I know now how then she showed me
Her mind, reaching out to the horizon,
She close above the tree tops.
I saw her eyes straining at the new distance
And as the woods fell from her flying
Likewise they fell from me as I followed
So that I strongly guessed all that I must put from me
To come through ready for the high courses.

But one day, crossing the ferry
With the great towers of Manhattan before me,
Out at the prow with the sea wind blowing,
I had been wearying many questions
Which she had put on to try me:
How shall I be a mirror to this modernity?
When lo! in a rush, dragging
A blunt boat on the yielding river—
Suddenly I saw her! And she waved me
From the white wet in midst of her playing!
She cried me, "Haia! Here I am, son!
See how strong my little finger is!
Can I not swim well?
I can fly too!" And with that a great sea-gull
Went to the left, vanishing with a wild cry—
But in my mind all the persons of godhead
Followed after.

3

CLARITY

"Come!" cried my mind and by her might
That was upon us we flew above the river
Seeking her, grey gulls among the white—
In the air speaking as she had willed it;
"I am given," cried I, "now I know it!
I know now all my time is forespent!
For me one face is all the world!
For I have seen her at last, this day,
In whom age in age is united—
Indifferent, out of sequence, marvelously!
Saving alone that one sequence
Which is the beauty of all the world, for surely
Either there in the rolling smoke spheres below us
Or here with us in the air intercircling,
Certainly somewhere here about us
I know she is revealing these things!"
And as gulls we flew and with soft cries
We seemed to speak, flying, "It is she
The mighty, recreating the whole world,
This is the first day of wonders!

She is attiring herself before me—
Taking shape before me for worship,
A red leaf that falls upon a stone!
It is she of whom I told you, old
Forgiveless, unreconcilable;
That high wanderer of by-ways
Walking imperious in beggary!
At her throat is loose gold, a single chain
From among many, on her bent fingers
Are rings from which the stones are fallen,
Her wrists wear a diminished state, her ankles
Are bare! Toward the river! Is it she there?"
And we swerved clamorously downward—
"I will take my peace in her henceforth!"

4

BROADWAY

It was then she struck—from behind,
In mid air, as with the edge of a great wing!
And instantly down the mists of my eyes
There came crowds walking—men as visions
With expressionless, animate faces;
Empty men with shell-thin bodies
Jostling close above the gutter,
Hasting—nowhere! And then for the first time
I really saw her, really scented the sweat
Of her presence and—fell back sickened!
Ominous, old, painted—
With bright lips, and lewd Jew's eyes
Her might strapped in by a corset
To give her age youth, perfect
In her will to be young she had covered
The godhead to go beside me.
Silent, her voice entered at my eyes
And my astonished thought followed her easily:
"Well, do their eyes shine, do their clothes fit?
These live I tell you! Old men with red cheeks,
Young men in gay suits! See them!
Dogged, quivering, impassive—
Well—are these the ones you envied?"
At which I answered her, "Marvelous old queen,
Grant me power to catch something of this day's
Air and sun into your service!
That these toilers after peace and after pleasure
May turn to you, worshippers at all hours!"
But she sniffed upon the words warily—
Yet I persisted, watching for an answer:
"To you, horrible old woman,
Who know all fires out of the bodies
Of all men that walk with lust at heart!
To you, O mighty, crafty prowler

5

After the youth of all cities, drunk
With the sight of thy archness! All the youth
That come to you, you having the knowledge
Rather than to those uninitiate—
To you, marvelous old queen, give me always
A new marriage—"
                        But she laughed loudly—
"A new grip upon those garments that brushed me
In days gone by on beach, lawn, and in forest!
May I be lifted still, up and out of terror,
Up from before the death living around me—
Torn up continually and carried
Whatever way the head of your whim is,
A burr upon those streaming tatters—"
But the night had fallen, she stilled me
And led me away.

THE STRIKE

At the first peep of dawn she roused me!
I rose trembling at the change which the night saw!
For there, wretchedly brooding in a corner
From which her old eyes glittered fiercely—
"Go!" she said, and I hurried shivering
Out into the deserted streets of Paterson.
That night she came again, hovering
In rags within the filmy ceiling—
"Great Queen, bless me with thy tatters!"
"You are blest, go on!"
                        "Hot for savagery,
Sucking the air! I went into the city,
Out again, baffled onto the mountain!
Back into the city!
                        Nowhere
The subtle! Everywhere the electric!"

6

"A short bread-line before a hitherto empty tea shop:
No questions—all stood patiently,
Dominated by one idea: something
That carried them as they are always wanting to be carried,
'But what is it,' I asked those nearest me,
'This thing heretofore unobtainable
'That they seem so clever to have put on now!'

"Why since I have failed them can it be anything but their
     own brood?
Can it be anything but brutality?
On that at least they're united! That at least
Is their bean soup, their calm bread and a few luxuries!

"But in me, more sensitive, marvelous old queen
It sank deep into the blood, that I rose upon
The tense air enjoying the dusty fight!
Heavy drink where the low, sloping foreheads
The flat skulls with the unkempt black or blond hair,
The ugly legs of the young girls, pistons
Too powerful for delicacy!
The women's wrists, the men's arms red
Used to heat and cold, to toss quartered beeves
And barrels, and milk-cans, and crates of fruit!

"Faces all knotted up like burls on oaks,
Grasping, fox-snouted, thick-lipped,
Sagging breasts and protruding stomachs,
Rasping voices, filthy habits with the hands.
Nowhere you! Everywhere the electric!

"Ugly, venomous, gigantic!
Tossing me as a great father his helpless
Infant till it shriek with ecstasy
And its eyes roll and its tongue hangs out!—

"I am at peace again, old queen, I listen clearer now."

7

ABROAD

Never, even in a dream,
Have I winged so high nor so well
As with her, she leading me by the hand,
That first day on the Jersey mountains!
And never shall I forget
The trembling interest with which I heard
Her voice in a low thunder:
"You are safe here. Look child, look open-mouth!
The patch of road between the steep bramble banks;
The tree in the wind, the white house there, the sky!
Speak to men of these, concerning me!
For never while you permit them to ignore me
In these shall the full of my freed voice
Come grappling the ear with intent!
Never while the air's clear coolness
Is seized to be a coat for pettiness;
Never while richness of greenery
Stands a shield for prurient minds;
Never, permitting these things unchallenged
Shall my voice of leaves and varicolored bark come free
    through!"
At which, knowing her solitude,
I shouted over the country below me:
"Waken! my people, to the boughs green
With ripening fruit within you!
Waken to the myriad cinquefoil
In the waving grass of your minds!
Waken to the silent phoebe nest
Under the eaves of your spirit!"

But she, stooping nearer the shifting hills
Spoke again. "Look there! See them!
There in the oat field with the horses,
See them there! bowed by their passions

Crushed down, that had been raised as a roof beam!
The weight of the sky is upon them
Under which all roof beams crumble.
There is none but the single roof beam:
There is no love bears against the great firefly!"
At this I looked up at the sun
Then shouted again with all the might I had.
But my voice was a seed in the wind.
Then she, the old one, laughing
Seized me and whirling about bore back
To the city, upward, still laughing
Until the great towers stood above the marshland
Wheeling beneath: the little creeks, the mallows
That I picked as a boy, the Hackensack
So quiet that seemed so broad formerly:
The crawling trains, the cedar swamp on the one side—
All so old, so familiar—so new now
To my marvelling eyes as we passed
Invisible.

SOOTHSAY

Eight days went by, eight days
Comforted by no nights, until finally:
"Would you behold yourself old, beloved?"
I was pierced, yet I consented gladly
For I knew it could not be otherwise.
And she—"Behold yourself old!
Sustained in strength, wielding might in gript surges!
Not bodying the sun in weak leaps
But holding way over rockish men
With fern-free fingers on their little crags,
Their hollows, the new Atlas, to bear them
For pride and for mockery! Behold
Yourself old! winding with slow might—
A vine among oaks—to the thin tops:

9

Leaving the leafless leaved,
Bearing purple clusters! Behold
Yourself old! birds are behind you.
You are the wind coming that stills birds,
Shakes the leaves in booming polyphony—
Slow winning high way amid the knocking
Of boughs, evenly crescendo,
The din and bellow of the male wind!
Leap then from forest into foam!
Lash about from low into high flames
Tipping sound, the female chorus—
Linking all lions, all twitterings
To make them nothing! Behold yourself old!"
As I made to answer she continued,
A little wistfully yet in a voice clear cut:
"Good is my over lip and evil
My under lip to you henceforth:
For I have taken your soul between my two hands
And this shall be as it is spoken."

ST. JAMES' GROVE

And so it came to that last day
When, she leading by the hand, we went out
Early in the morning, I heavy of heart
For I knew the novitiate was ended
The ecstasy was over, the life begun.
In my woolen shirt and the pale-blue necktie
My grandmother gave me, there I went
With the old queen right past the houses
Of my friends down the hill to the river
As on any usual day, any errand.
Alone, walking under trees,
I went with her, she with me in her wild hair,
By Santiago Grove and presently
She bent forward and knelt by the river,

10

The Passaic, that filthy river.
And there dabbling her mad hands,
She called me close beside her.
Raising the water then in the cupped palm
She bathed our brows wailing and laughing:
"River, we are old, you and I,
We are old and by bad luck, beggars.
Lo, the filth in our hair, our bodies stink!
Old friend, here I have brought you
The young soul you long asked of me.
Stand forth, river, and give me
The old friend of my revels!
Give me the well-worn spirit,
For here I have made a room for it,
And I will return to you forthwith
The youth you have long asked of me:
Stand forth, river, and give me
The old friend of my revels!"

And the filthy Passaic consented!

Then she, leaping up with a fierce cry:
"Enter, youth, into this bulk!
Enter, river, into this young man!"
Then the river began to enter my heart,
Eddying back cool and limpid
Into the crystal beginning of its days.
But with the rebound it leaped forward:
Muddy, then black and shrunken
Till I felt the utter depth of its rottenness
The vile breadth of its degradation
And dropped down knowing this was me now.
But she lifted me and the water took a new tide
Again into the older experiences,
And so, backward and forward,
It tortured itself within me

Until time had been washed finally under,
And the river had found its level
And its last motion had ceased
And I knew all—it became me.
And I knew this for double certain
For there, whitely, I saw myself
Being borne off under the water!
I could have shouted out in my agony
At the sight of myself departing
Forever—but I bit back my despair
For she had averted her eyes
By which I knew well what she was thinking—
And so the last of me was taken.

Then she, "Be mostly silent!"
And turning to the river, spoke again:
"For him and for me, river, the wandering,
But by you I leave for happiness
Deep foliage, the thickest beeches—
Though elsewhere they are all dying—
Tallest oaks and yellow birches
That dip their leaves in you, mourning,
As now I dip my hair, immemorial
Of me, immemorial of him
Immemorial of these our promises!
Here shall be a bird's paradise,
They sing to you remembering my voice:
Here the most secluded spaces
For miles around, hallowed by a stench
To be our joint solitude and temple;
In memory of this clear marriage
And the child I have brought you in the late years.
Live, river, live in luxuriance
Remembering this our son,
In remembrance of me and my sorrow
And of the new wandering!"

The Tempers

The Tempest

Peace on Earth

The archer is wake!
The Swan is flying!
Gold against blue
An Arrow is lying.
There is hunting in heaven—
Sleep safe till tomorrow.

The Bears are abroad!
The Eagle is screaming!
Gold against blue
Their eyes are gleaming!
Sleep!
Sleep safe till tomorrow.

The Sisters lie
With their arms intertwining;
Gold against blue
Their hair is shining!
The Serpent writhes!
Orion is listening!
Gold against blue
His sword is glistening!
Sleep!
There is hunting in heaven—
Sleep safe till tomorrow.

Postlude

Now that I have cooled to you
Let there be gold of tarnished masonry,
Temples soothed by the sun to ruin
That sleep utterly.
Give me hand for the dances,
Ripples at Philae, in and out,
And lips, my Lesbian,
Wall flowers that once were flame.

Your hair is my Carthage
And my arms the bow,
And our words arrows
To shoot the stars
Who from that misty sea
Swarm to destroy us.
But you there beside me—
Oh how shall I defy you,
Who wound me in the night
With breasts shining
Like Venus and like Mars?
The night that is shouting Jason
When the loud eaves rattle
As with waves above me
Blue at the prow of my desire.

O, prayers in the dark!
O, incense to Poseidon!
Calm in Atlantis.

First Praise

Lady of dusk-wood fastnesses,
    Thou art my Lady.
I have known the crisp, splintering leaf-tread with thee on
        before,
White, slender through green saplings;
I have lain by thee on the brown forest floor
    Beside thee, my Lady.

Lady of rivers strewn with stones,
    Only thou art my Lady.
Where thousand the freshets are crowded like peasants to
        a fair;
Clear-skinned, wild from seclusion
They jostle white-armed down the tent-bordered
        thoroughfare
    Praising my Lady.

Homage

Elvira, by love's grace
There goeth before you
A clear radiance
Which maketh all vain souls
Candles when noon is.

The loud clangor of pretenders
Melteth before you
Like the roll of carts passing,
But you come silently
And homage is given.

Now the little by-path
Which leadeth to love
Is again joyful with its many;
And the great highway
From love
Is without passers.

The Fool's Song

I tried to put a bird in a cage.
O fool that I am!
For the bird was Truth.
Sing merrily, Truth: I tried to put
Truth in a cage!

And when I had the bird in the cage,
O fool that I am!
Why, it broke my pretty cage.
Sing merrily, Truth: I tried to put
Truth in a cage!

And when the bird was flown from the cage,
O fool that I am!
Why, I had nor bird nor cage.
Sing merrily, Truth: I tried to put
Truth in a cage!
Heigh-ho! Truth in a cage.

From "The Birth of Venus", Song

Come with us and play!
See, we have breasts as women!
From your tents by the sea
Come play with us: it is forbidden!

Come with us and play!
Lo, bare, straight legs in the water!
By our boats we stay,
Then swimming away
Come to us: it is forbidden!

Come with us and play!
See, we are tall as women!
Our eyes are keen:
Our hair is bright:
Our voices speak outright:
We revel in the sea's green!
Come play:
It is forbidden!

Immortal

Yes, there is one thing braver than all flowers;
  Richer than clear gems; wider than the sky;
Immortal and unchangeable; whose powers
  Transcend reason, love and sanity!

And thou, beloved, art that godly thing!
  Marvelous and terrible; in glance
An injured Juno roused against Heaven's King!
  And thy name, lovely One, is Ignorance.

Mezzo Forte

Take that, damn you; and that!
    And here's a rose
  To make it right again!
    God knows
  I'm sorry, Grace; but then,
It's not my fault if you will be a cat.

Crude Lament

            Mother of flames,
            The men that went ahunting
Are asleep in the snow drifts.
            You have kept the fire burning!
Crooked fingers that pull
Fuel from among the wet leaves,
            Mother of flames
            You have kept the fire burning!
The young wives have fallen asleep
With wet hair, weeping,
            Mother of flames!
The young men raised the heavy spears
And are gone prowling in the darkness.
            O mother of flames,
            You who have kept the fire burning!
            Lo, I am helpless!
Would God they had taken me with them!

An After Song

So art thou broken in upon me, Apollo,
Through a splendor of purple garments—
Held by the yellow-haired Clymene
To clothe the white of thy shoulders—
Bare from the day's leaping of horses.
This is strange to me, here in the modern twilight.

The Ordeal

O crimson salamander,
Because of love's whim
                    sacred!
Swim
    the winding flame
    Predestined to disman him
And bring our fellow home to us again.
    Swim in with watery fang,
    Gnaw out and drown
The fire roots that circle him
Until the Hell-flower dies down
    And he comes home again.

Aye, bring him home,
    O crimson salamander,
That I may see he is unchanged with burning—
Then have your will with him,
    O crimson salamander.

Appeal

You who are so mighty,
crimson salamander,
hear me once more.
I lay among the half-burned sticks
at the edge of the fire.
The fiend was creeping in.
I felt the cold tips of fingers—

O crimson salamander!

Give me one little flame,
one!
that I may bind it
protectingly about the wrist
of him that flung me here,
here upon the very center!

This is my song.

Fire Spirit

I am old.
You warm yourselves at these fires?
In the center of these flames
I sit, my teeth chatter!
Where shall I turn for comfort?

24

The Death of Franco of Cologne:
His Prophecy of Beethoven

It is useless, good woman, useless: the spark fails me.
God! yet when the might of it all assails me
It seems impossible that I cannot do it.
Yet I cannot. They were right, and they all knew it
Years ago, but I—never! I have persisted
Blindly (they say) and now I am old. I have resisted
Everything, but now, now the strife's ended.
The fire's out; the old cloak has been mended
For the last time, the soul peers through its tatters.
Put a light by and leave me; nothing more matters
Now; I am done; I am at last well broken!
Yet, by God, I'll still leave them a token
That they'll swear it was no dead man writ it;
A morsel that they'll mark well the day they bit it,
That there'll be sand between their gross teeth to crunch yet
When goodman Gabriel blows his concluding trumpet.
Leave me!
                · And now, little black eyes, come you out here!
Ah, you've given me a lively, lasting bout, year
After year to win you round me darlings!
Precious children, little gambollers! "farlings"
They might have called you once, "nearlings"
I call you now, I first of all the yearlings,
Upon this plain, for I it was that tore you
Out of chaos! It was I bore you!
Ah, you little children that go playing
Over the five-barred gate, and will still be straying
Spite of all that I have ever told you
Of counterpoint and cadence which does not hold you—
No more than chains will for this or that strange reason,
But you're always at some new loving treason

To be away from me, laughing, mocking,
Witlessly, perhaps, but for all that forever knocking
At this stanchion door of your poor father's heart till—
    oh, well
At least you've shown that you can grow well
However much you evade me faster, faster.
But, black eyes some day you'll get a master,
For he will come! He shall, he must come!
And when he finishes and the burning dust from
His wheels settles—what shall men see then?
You, you, you, my own lovely children!
Aye, all of you, thus with hands together
Playing on the hill or there in a tether,
Or running free, but all mine! Aye, my very namesakes
Shall be his proper fame's stakes.
And he shall lead you!
And he shall mead you!
And he shall build you gold palaces!
And he shall wine you from clear chalices!
For I have seen it! I have seen it
Written where the world-clouds screen it
From other eyes
Over the bronze gates of paradise!

Portent

Red cradle of the night,
In you
The dusky child
Sleeps fast till his might
Shall be piled
Sinew on sinew.

Red cradle of the night,
The dusky child
Sleeping sits upright.
Lo! how
The winds blow now!
He pillows back;
The winds are again mild.

When he stretches his arms out,
Red cradle of the night,
The alarms shout
From bare tree to tree,
Wild
In afright!
Mighty shall he be,
Red cradle of the night,
The dusky child! !

Ad Infinitum

> Still I bring flowers
> Although you fling them at my feet
> Until none stays
> That is not struck across with wounds:
> Flowers and flowers
> That you may break them utterly
> As you have always done.
>
> Sure happily
> I still bring flowers, flowers,
> Knowing how all
> Are crumpled in your praise
> And may not live
> To speak a lesser thing.

Contemporania

The corner of a great rain
Steamy with the country
Has fallen upon my garden.

I go back and forth now
And the little leaves follow me
Talking of the great rain,
Of branches broken,
And the farmer's curses!

But I go back and forth
In this corner of a garden
And the green shoots follow me
Praising the great rain.

We are not curst together,
The leaves and I,
Framing devices, flower devices
And other ways of peopling
The barren country.
Truly it was a very great rain
That makes the little leaves follow me.

Hic Jacet

The coroner's merry little children
    Have such twinkling brown eyes.
Their father is not of gay men
    And their mother jocular in no wise,
Yet the coroner's merry little children
    Laugh so easily.

They laugh because they prosper.
    Fruit for them is upon all branches.
Lo! how they jibe at loss, for
    Kind heaven fills their little paunches!
It's the coroner's merry, merry children
    Who laugh so easily.

Con Brio

Miserly, is the best description of that poor fool
Who holds Lancelot to have been a morose fellow,
Dolefully brooding over the events which had naturally
    to follow
The high time of his deed with Guinevere.
He has a sick historical sight, if I judge rightly,
To believe any such thing as that ever occurred.
But, by the god of blood, what else is it that has deterred
Us all from an out and out defiance of fear
But this same perdamnable miserliness,
Which cries about our necks how we shall have less
    and less
Than we have now if we spend too wantonly?
Bah, this sort of slither is below contempt!
In the same vein we should have apple trees exempt
From bearing anything but pink blossoms all the year,
Fixed permanent lest their bellies wax unseemly, and the dear
Innocent days of them be wasted quite.
How can we have less? Have we not the deed?
Lancelot thought little, spent his gold and rode to fight
Mounted, if God was willing, on a good steed.

To Wish Myself Courage

On the day when youth is no more upon me
I will write of the leaves and the moon in a tree top!
I will sing then the song, long in the making—
When the stress of youth is put away from me.

How can I ever be written out as men say?
Surely it is merely an interference with the long song—
This that I am now doing.

But when the spring of it is worn like the old moon
And the eaten leaves are lace upon the cold earth—
Then I will rise up in my great desire—
Long at the birth—and sing me the youth-song!

To Mark Anthony in Heaven

This quiet morning light
reflected, how many times
from grass and trees and clouds
enters my north room
touching the walls with
grass and clouds and trees.
Anthony,
trees and grass and clouds.
Why did you follow
that beloved body
with your ships at Actium?
I hope it was because
you knew her inch by inch
from slanting feet upward
to the roots of her hair
and down again and that
you saw her
above the battle's fury—
clouds and trees and grass—

For then you are
listening in heaven.

Transitional

First he said:
It is the woman in us
That makes us write—
Let us acknowledge it—
Men would be silent.
We are not men
Therefore we can speak
And be conscious
(of the two sides)
Unbent by the sensual
As befits accuracy.

I then said:
Dare you make this
Your propaganda?

And he answered:
Am I not I—here?

Sicilian Emigrant's Song

O—eh—lee! La—la!
    Donna! Donna!
Blue is the sky of Palermo;
Blue is the little bay;
And dost thou remember the orange and fig,
The lively sun and the sea-breeze at evening?
      Hey—la!
Donna! Donna! Maria!

O—eh—li! La—la!
    Donna! Donna!
Grey is the sky of this land.
Grey and green is the water.
I see no trees, dost thou? The wind
Is cold for the big woman there with the candle
      Hey—la!
Donna! Donna! Maria!

O—eh—li! O—la!
    Donna! Donna!
I sang thee by the blue waters;
I sing thee here in the grey dawning.
Kiss, for I put down my guitar;
I'll sing thee more songs after the landing.
     O Jesu, I love thee!
Donna! Donna! Maria!

Le Medecin Malgre Lui

Oh I suppose I should
wash the walls of my office
polish the rust from
my instruments and keep them
definitely in order
build shelves in the laboratory
empty out the old stains
clean the bottles
and refill them, buy
another lens, put
my journals on edge instead of
letting them lie flat
in heaps—then begin
ten years back and
gradually
read them to date
cataloguing important
articles for ready reference.
I suppose I should
read the new books.
If to this I added
a bill at the tailor's
and at the cleaner's
grew a decent beard
and cultivated a look
of importance—
Who can tell? I might be
a credit to my Lady Happiness
and never think anything
but a white thought!

Man in a Room

Here, no woman, nor man besides,
Nor child, nor dog, nor bird, nor wasp,
Nor ditch-pool, nor green thing. Color of flower,
Blood-bright berry none, nor flame-rust
On leaf, nor pink gall-sting on stem, nor
Staring stone, *Ay de mi!*
No hawthorn's white thorn-tree here, nor lawn
Of buttercups, nor any counterpart:

Bed, book-backs, walls, floor,
Flat pictures, desk, clothes-box, litter
Of paper scrawls. So sit I here,
So stand, so walk about. Beside
The flower-white tree not so lonely I:
Torn petals, dew-wet, yellowed my bare ankles.

A Coronal

New books of poetry will be written
New books and unheard of manuscripts
will come wrapped in brown paper
and many and many a time
the postman will blow
and sidle down the leaf-plastered steps
thumbing over other men's business

But we ran ahead of it all.
One coming after
could have seen her footprints
in the wet and followed us
among the stark chestnuts.

Anemones sprang where she pressed
and cresses
stood green in the slender source—
And new books of poetry
will be written, leather-colored oakleaves
many and many a time.

The Revelation

I awoke happy, the house
Was strange, voices
Were across a gap
Through which a girl
Came and paused,
Reaching out to me—

Then I remembered
What I had dreamed—
A girl
One whom I knew well
Leaned on the door of my car
And stroked my hand—

I shall pass her on the street
We shall say trivial things
To each other
But I shall never cease
To search her eyes
For that quiet look—

Portrait of a Lady

Your thighs are appletrees
whose blossoms touch the sky.
Which sky? The sky
where Watteau hung a lady's
slipper. Your knees
are a southern breeze—or
a gust of snow. Agh! what
sort of man was Fragonard?
—as if that answered
anything. Ah, yes—below
the knees, since the tune
drops that way, it is
one of those white summer days,
the tall grass of your ankles
flickers upon the shore—
Which shore?—
the sand clings to my lips—
Which shore?
Agh, petals maybe. How
should I know?
Which shore? Which shore?
I said petals from an appletree.

March

•

History

March

I

Winter is long in this climate
and spring—a matter of a few days
only,—a flower or two picked
from mud or from among wet leaves
or at best against treacherous
bitterness of wind, and sky shining
teasingly, then closing in black
and sudden, with fierce jaws.

II

March,
    you remind me of
the pyramids, our pyramids—
stript of the polished stone
that used to guard them!
                        March,
you are like Fra Angelico
at Fiesole, painting on plaster!

March,
    you are like a band of
young poets that have not learned
the blessedness of warmth
(or have forgotten it).
At any rate—
I am moved to write poetry
for the warmth there is in it
and for the loneliness—
a poem that shall have you
    in it March.

43

III

See!
    Ashur-ban-i-pal,
the archer king, on horse-back,
in blue and yellow enamel!
with drawn bow—facing lions
standing on their hind legs,
fangs bared! his shafts
bristling in their necks!

Sacred bulls—dragons
in embossed brickwork
marching—in four tiers—
along the sacred way to
Nebuchadnessar's throne hall!
They shine in the sun,
they that have been marching—
marching under the dust of
ten thousand dirt years.

Now—
they are coming into bloom again!
See them!
marching still, bared by
the storms from my calendar
—winds that blow back the sand!
winds that enfilade dirt!
winds that by strange craft
have whipt up a black army
that by pick and shovel
bare a procession to
                the god, Marduk!

Natives cursing and digging
for pay unearth dragons with
upright tails and sacred bulls

alternately—
                in four tiers—
lining the way to an old altar!
Natives digging at old walls—
digging me warmth—digging me sweet loneliness
high enamelled walls.

                            IV

My second spring—
passed in a monastery
with plaster walls—in Fiesole
on the hill above Florence.
My second spring—painted
a virgin—in a blue aureole
sitting on a three-legged stool,
arms crossed—
she is intently serious,
                            and still

watching an angel
with colored wings
half kneeling before her—
and smiling—the angel's eyes
holding the eyes of Mary
as a snake's hold a bird's.
On the ground there are flowers,
trees are in leaf.

                            V

But! now for the battle!
Now for murder—now for the real thing!
My third springtime is approaching!
Winds!

lean, serious as a virgin,
seeking, seeking the flowers of March.
Seeking
flowers nowhere to be found,
they twine among the bare branches
in insatiable eagerness—
they whirl up the snow
seeking under it—
they—the winds—snakelike
roar among yellow reeds
seeking flowers—flowers.

I spring among them
seeking one flower
in which to warm myself!

I deride with all the ridicule
of misery—
my own starved misery.

Counter-cutting winds strike against me
refreshing their fury!

Come, good, cold fellows!
    Have we no flowers?
Defy then with even more
desperation than ever—being
    lean and frozen!

But though you are lean and frozen—
think of the blue bulls of Babylon.
Fling yourselves upon
    their empty roses—
        cut savagely!

But—
think of the painted monastery
    at Fiesole.

History

History

A wind might blow a lotus petal
over the pyramids—but not this wind.

Summer is a dried leaf.

Leaves stir this way then that
on the baked asphalt, the wheels
of motor cars rush over them,—
    gas smells mingle with leaf smells.

Oh, Sunday, day of worship! ! !

The steps to the Museum are high.
Worshippers pass in and out.
Nobody comes here today.
I come here to mingle faïence dug
from the tomb, turquoise-colored
necklaces and wind belched from the
stomach; deliberately veined basins
of agate, cracked and discolored and
the stink of stale urine!

Enter! Elbow in at the door.
Men? Women?
Simpering, clay fetish-faces counting
through the turnstile.
              Ah!

This sarcophagus contained the body
of Uresh-Nai, priest to the goddess Mut,
Mother of All—

Run your finger against this edge!
—here went the chisel!—and think
of an arrogance endured six thousand
    years
Without a flaw!

But love is an oil to embalm the body.
Love is a packet of spices, a strong-
smelling liquid to be squirted into
the thigh. No?
Love rubbed on a bald head will make
hair—and after? Love is
a lice comber!
                Gnats on dung!

"The chisel is in your hand, the block
is before you, cut as I shall dictate:
This is the coffin of Uresh-Nai,
priest to the Sky Goddess,—built
to endure forever!
             Carve the inside
with the image of my death in
little lines of figures three fingers high.
Put a lid on it cut with Mut bending over
the earth, for my headpiece, and in
    the year
to be chosen I shall rouse, the lid
shall be lifted and I will walk about
the temple where they have rested me

and eat the air of the place:
Ah—these walls are high! This is in
keeping."

3

The priest has passed into his tomb.
The stone has taken up his spirit!
Granite over the flesh: who will deny
its advantages?

Your death?—water
spilled upon the ground—
though water will mount again into
rose-leaves—
but you?—Would hold life still,
even as a memory, when it is over,
Benevolence is rare.

Climb about this sarcophagus, read
what is writ for you in these figures
hard as the granite that has held them
with so soft a hand the while
your own flesh has been fifty times
through the guts of oxen,—read!
"I who am the one flesh say to you,
The rose-tree will have its donor
even though he give stingily.
The gift of some endures
ten years, the gift of some twenty
and the gift of some for the time a
great house rots and is torn down.
Some give for a thousand years to
men of
one face, some for a thousand

to all men and some few to all men
while granite holds an edge against
the weather.
    Judge then of love!"

4

"My flesh is turned to stone. I
have endured my summer. The flurry
of falling petals is ended. Lay
the finger upon this granite. I was
well desired and fully caressed
by many lovers but my flesh
withered swiftly and my heart was
never satisfied. Lay your hands
upon the granite as a lover lays his
hand upon the thigh and upon the
round breasts of her who is beside
him, for now I will not wither,
now I have thrown off secrecy, now
I have walked naked into the street,
now I have scattered my heavy beauty
in the open market.
Here I am with head high and a
burning heart eagerly awaiting
your caresses, whoever it may be,
for granite is not harder than my
love is open, runs loose among you!

I arrogant against death! I
who have endured! I worn against
the years!"

5

But it is five o'clock. Come!
Life is good—enjoy it!
A walk in the park while the day lasts.
I will go with you. Look! this
northern scenery is not the Nile, but—
these benches—the yellow and purple
        dusk—
the moon there—these tired people—
the lights on the water!

Are not these Jews and—Ethiopians?
The world is young, surely! Young
and colored like—a girl that has come
        upon
a lover! Will that do?

Della Primavera Transportata Al Morale

Della Primavera Trasportata Al Morale

APRIL

the beginning—or
what you will:
                    the dress
in which the veritable winter
walks in Spring—

Loose it!
Let it fall (where it will)
—again

A live thing
the buds are upon it
the green shoot come between
the red flowerets
                    curled back

Under whose green veil
strain trunk and limbs of
the supporting trees—

Yellow! the arched stick
pinning the fragile foil
—in abundance
                    or

the bush before the rose
pointed with green

bent into form
upon the iron frame

wild onion
swifter than the grass

the grass thick
at the post's base

iris blades unsheathed—

BUY THIS PROPERTY

—the complexion of the impossible
(you'll say)

never realized—
At a desk in a hotel in front of a

machine a year
later—for a day or two—

(Quite so—)
Whereas the reality trembles

frankly
in that though it was like this

in part
it was deformed

even when at its utmost to
touch—as it did

and fill and give and take
—a kind

of rough drawing of flowers
and April

STOP : GO

   —she
opened the door! nearly
six feet tall, and I . . .
wanted to found a new country—

For the rest, virgin negress
at the glass
in blue-glass Venetian beads—

     a green truck
     dragging a concrete mixer
     passes
     in the street—
     the clatter and true sound
     of verse—

—the wind is howling
the river, shining mud—

Moral
  it looses me

Moral
  it supports me

Moral
  it has never ceased
  to flow

Moral
  the faded evergreen

Moral
  I can laugh

Moral
>the redhead sat
>in bed with her legs
>crossed and talked
>rough stuff

Moral
>the door is open

Moral
>the tree moving diversely
>in all parts—

—the moral is love, bred of
the mind and eyes and hands—

>But in the cross-current

>between what the hands reach
>and the mind desires

>and the eyes see
>and see starvation, it is

>useless to have it thought
>that we are full—

>But April is a thing
>comes just the same—

>and in it we see now
>what then we did not know—

STOP : STOP

I believe
>in the sound patriotic and

progressive Mulish policies
and if elected—

I believe
     in a continuance of the pro-
     tective tariff because—

I believe
     that the country can't do
     too much—

I believe
     in honest law enforcement—
     and I also believe—

I believe
     in giving the farmer and
     land owner adequate protection

I believe

I believe

I believe
     in equality for the negro—

          THIS IS MY PLATFORM

     I believe in your love

     the first dandelion
     flower at the edge of—

taraaaaaaa!   taraaaaaaa!

—the fishman's bugle announces
the warm wind—

reminiscent of the sea
the plumtree flaunts
its blossom-encrusted
branches—

I believe
    Moving to three doors
    above—May 1st.

I believe
    ICE—and warehouse site

No parking between tree and corner

You would "kill me with kindness"
I love you too, but I love you
too—

Thus, in that light and in that
light only can I say—

Winter : Spring
abandoned to you. The world lost—
in you

Is not that devastating enough
for one century?

I believe
    Spumoni $1.00
    French Vanilla   .70
    Chocolate   .70
    Strawberry   .70
    Maple Walnut   .70
    Coffee   .70
    Tutti Frutti   .70

```
Pistachio              .70
Cherry Special         .70
Orange Ice             .70
Biscuit Tortoni
              25c per portion
```

trees—seeming dead:
      the long years—

tactus eruditus

    Maple, I see you have
    a squirrel in your crotch—

    And you have a woodpecker
    in your hole, Sycamore

—a fat blonde, in purple (no trucking
on this street)

POISON!

I believe

WOMAN'S WARD

PRIVATE

The soul, my God, shall rise up
—a tree

But who are You?
in this mortal wind
that I at least can understand
having sinned willingly

The forms
of the emotions are crystalline,
geometric-faceted. So we recognize
only in the white heat of
understanding, when a flame
runs through the gap made
by learning, the shapes of things—
the ovoid sun, the pointed trees

lashing branches

The wind is fierce, lashing

the long-limbed trees whose
branches
wildly toss—

Full Moon

Blessed moon
noon
of night

that through the dark
bids Love
stay—

curious shapes
awake
to plague me

Is day near
shining girl?
Yes, day!

the warm
the radiant
all fulfilling

day.

The Trees

The trees—being trees
thrash and scream
guffaw and curse—
wholly abandoned
damning the race of men—

Christ, the bastards
haven't even sense enough
to stay out of the rain—

Wha ha ha ha

Wheeeeee
Clacka tacka tacka
tacka tacka
wha ha ha ha ha
ha ha ha

knocking knees, buds
bursting from each pore
even the trunk's self
putting out leafheads—

Loose desire!
we naked cry to you—
"Do what you please."

You cannot!

—ghosts
sapped of strength

wailing at the gate
heartbreak at the bridgehead—

desire
dead in the heart

haw haw haw haw
—and memory broken

wheeeeee

There were never satyrs
never maenads
never eagle-headed gods—
These were men
from whose hands sprung
love
bursting the wood—

Trees their companions
—a cold wind winterlong
in the hollows of our flesh
icy with pleasure—

no part of us untouched

The Wind Increases

The harried
earth is swept
                    The trees
the tulip's bright
            tips
                    sidle and
toss—

            Loose your love
to flow

Blow!

Good Christ what is
a poet—if any
                    exists?

a man
whose words will
            bite
                    their way
home—being actual

having the form
                    of motion

At each twigtip

new

upon the tortured
body of thought

           gripping
     the ground

  a way
       to the last leaftip

The Bird's Companion

As love
     that is
each day upon the twig
    which may die

     So springs your love
fresh up
    lusty for the sun
the bird's companion—

The House

The house is yours
to wander in as you please—
Your breakfasts will be kept
ready for you until

you choose to arise!
This is the front room
where we stood penniless
by the hogshead of crockery.

This is the kitchen—
We have a new
hotwater heater and a new
gas-stove to please you

And the front stairs
have been freshly painted—
white risers
and the treads mahogany.

Come upstairs
to the bedroom—
Your bed awaits you—
the chiffonier waits—

the whole house
is waiting—for you
to walk in it at your pleasure—
It is yours.

The Sea-Elephant

Trundled from
the strangeness of the sea—
a kind of
heaven—

Ladies and Gentlemen!
the greatest
sea-monster ever exhibited
alive

the gigantic
sea-elephant! O wallow
of flesh were
are

there fish enough for
that
appetite stupidity
cannot lessen?

Sick
of April's smallness
the little
leaves—

Flesh has lief of you
enormous sea—
Speak!
Blouaugh! (feed

me) my
flesh is riven—

fish after fish into his maw
unswallowing

to let them glide down
gulching back
half spittle half
brine

the
troubled eyes—torn
from the sea.
(In

a practical voice) They
ought
to put it back where
it came from.

Gape.
Strange head—
told by old sailors—
rising

bearded
to the surface—and
the only
sense out of them

is that woman's
Yes
it's wonderful but they
ought to

put it
back into the sea where

it came from.
Blouaugh!

Swing—ride
walk
on wires—toss balls
stoop and

contort yourselves—
But I
am love. I am
from the sea—

Blouaugh!
there is no crime save
the too-heavy
body

the sea
held playfully—comes
to the surface
the water

boiling
about the head the cows
scattering
fish dripping from

the bounty
of . . . . and spring
they say
Spring is icummen in—

Rain

As the rain falls
so does
        your love

bathe every
           open
object of the world—

In houses
the priceless dry
            rooms
of illicit love
where we live
hear the wash of the
                rain—

There
        paintings
and fine
         metalware
woven stuffs—
all the whorishness
of our
        delight
sees
from its window

the spring wash
of your love
         the falling
rain—

The trees
are become

beasts fresh-risen
from the sea—
water

trickles
from the crevices of
their hides—

So my life is spent
                    to keep out love
with which
she rains upon

              the world

of spring

          drips

so spreads

          the words

far apart to let in

                    her love

And running in between

the drops

          the rain

is a kind physician

                    the rain
of her thoughts over

the ocean
            every

where

            walking with
invisible swift feet
over

            the helpless
                        waves—

Unworldly love
that has no hope
                        of the world

                        and that
cannot change the world
to its delight—

            The rain
falls upon the earth
and grass and flowers

come
            perfectly

into form from its
                        liquid

clearness

            But love is
unworldly

            and nothing
comes of it but love

following
and falling endlessly
from
        her thoughts

Death

He's dead
the dog won't have to
sleep on his potatoes
any more to keep them
from freezing

he's dead
the old bastard—
He's a bastard because

there's nothing
legitimate in him any
more
        he's dead
He's sick-dead

                he's
a godforsaken curio
without
any breath in it

He's nothing at all
        he's dead
shrunken up to skin

      Put his head on
one chair and his
feet on another and
he'll lie there
like an acrobat—

Love's beaten. He
beat it. That's why
he's insufferable—

          because
he's here needing a
shave and making love
an inside howl
of anguish and defeat—

He's come out of the man
and he's let
the man go—
                    the liar

Dead
          his eyes
rolled up out of
the light—a mockery

                                        which
love cannot touch—

just bury it
and hide its face
for shame.

The Botticellian Trees

The alphabet of
the trees

is fading in the
song of the leaves

the crossing
bars of the thin

letters that spelled
winter

and the cold
have been illumined

with
pointed green

by the rain and sun—
The strict simple

principles of
straight branches

are being modified
by pinched-out

ifs of color, devout
conditions

the smiles of love—
. . . . . .

until the stript
sentences

move as a woman's
limbs under cloth

and praise from secrecy
quick with desire

love's ascendancy
in summer—

In summer the song
sings itself

above the muffled words—

An Early Martyr

An Early Martyr

Rather than permit him
to testify in court
Giving reasons
why he stole from
Exclusive stores
then sent post-cards
To the police
to come and arrest him
—if they could—
They railroaded him
to an asylum for
The criminally insane
without trial

The prophylactic to
madness
Having been denied him
he went close to
The edge out of
frustration and
Doggedness—

Inflexible, finally they
had to release him—
The institution was
"overcrowded"
They let him go
in the custody of
A relative on condition
that he remain
Out of the state—

They "cured" him all
right

But the set-up
he fought against
Remains—
and his youthful deed
Signalizing
the romantic period
Of a revolt
he served well
Is still good—

Let him be
a factory whistle
That keeps blaring—
Sense, sense, sense!
so long as there's
A mind to remember
and a voice to
carry it on—

Never give up
keep at it!
Unavoided, terrifying
to such bought
Courts as he thought
to trust to but they
Double-crossed him.

Flowers by the Sea

When over the flowery, sharp pasture's
edge, unseen, the salt ocean

lifts its form—chicory and daisies
tied, released, seem hardly flowers alone

but color and the movement—or the shape
perhaps—of restlessness, whereas

the sea is circled and sways
peacefully upon its plantlike stem

Wild Orchard

It is a broken country,
the rugged land is
green from end to end;
the autumn has not come.

Embanked above the orchard
the hillside is a wall
of motionless green trees,
the grass is green and red.

Five days the bare sky
has stood there day and night.
No bird, no sound.
Between the trees

stillness
and the early morning light.
The apple trees
are laden down with fruit.

Among blue leaves
the apples green and red
upon one tree stand out
most enshrined.

Still, ripe, heavy,
spherical and close,
they mark the hillside.
It is a formal grandeur,

a stateliness,
a signal of finality
and perfect ease.
Among the savage

aristocracy of rocks
one, risen as a tree,
has turned
from his repose.

Winter

Now the snow
lies on the ground
and more snow
is descending upon it—
Patches of red dirt
hold together
the old
snow patches

This is winter—
rosettes of
leather-green leaves
by the old fence
and bare trees
marking the sky—

This is winter
winter, winter
leather-green leaves
spearshaped
in the falling snow

The Flowers Alone

I should have to be
Chaucer to describe
them—
      Loss keeps
me from such a
catalogue—
But!
      —low, the
violet, scentless as
it is here! higher,
the peartree in full
bloom through which
a light falls as
rain—

And that is gone—

Only, there remains—

Now!
      the cherry trees
white in all back
yards—

      And bare as
they are, the coral
peach trees melting
the harsh air—
      excellence
priceless beyond
all later

      fruit!

And now, driven, I
go, forced to
another day—

Whose yellow quilt
flapping in the
stupendous light—

Forsythia, quince
blossoms—

and all
the living hybrids

Sea-Trout and Butterfish

The contours and the shine
hold the eye—caught and lying

orange-finned and the two
half its size, pout-mouthed

beside it on the white dish—
Silver scales, the weight

quick tails
whipping the streams aslant

The eye comes down eagerly
unravelled of the sea

separates this from that
and the fine fins' sharp spines

A Portrait of the Times

Two W. P. A. men
stood in the new
sluiceway

overlooking
the river—
One was pissing

while the other
showed
by his red

jagged face the
immemorial tragedy
of lack-love

while an old
squint-eyed woman
in a black

dress
and clutching
a bunch of

late chrysanthemums
to her
fatted bosoms

turned her back
on them
at the corner

The Locust Tree in Flower

Among
of
green

stiff
old
bright

broken
branch
come

white
sweet
May

again

The Locust Tree in Flower

Among
the leaves
bright

green
of wrist-thick
tree

and old
stiff broken
branch

ferncool
swaying
loosely strung—

come May
again
white blossom

clusters
hide
to spill

their sweets
almost
unnoticed

down
and quickly
fall

Item

This, with a face
like a mashed blood orange
that suddenly

would get eyes
and look up and scream
War! War!

clutching her
thick, ragged coat
A piece of hat

broken shoes
War! War!
stumbling for dread

at the young men
who with their gun-butts
shove her

sprawling—
a note
at the foot of the page

View of a Lake

from a
highway below a face
of rock

too recently blasted
to be overgrown
with grass or fern:

Where a
waste of cinders
slopes down to

the railroad and
the lake
stand three children

beside the weed-grown
chassis
of a wrecked car

immobile in a line
facing the water
To the left a boy

in falling off
blue overalls
Next to him a girl

in a grimy frock
And another boy
They are intent

watching something
below—?
A section sign: 50

on an iron post
planted
by a narrow concrete

service hut
(to which runs
a sheaf of wires)

in the universal
cinders beaten
into crossing paths

to form the front yard
of a frame house
at the right

that looks
to have been flayed
Opposite

remains a sycamore
in leaf
Intently fixed

the three
with straight backs
ignore

the stalled traffic
all eyes
toward the water

To a Mexican Pig-Bank

and a small
flock

of clay
sheep—

a shepherd
behind

them—The
pig

is painted
yellow

with green
ears

There's a
slot

at the
top—

Hair-pin
wires

hold up the
sheep

turning
away—

        The shepherd
            wears

        a red
            blanket

        on his left
            shoulder

To a Poor Old Woman

            munching a plum on
            the street a paper bag
            of them in her hand

            They taste good to her
            They taste good
            to her. They taste
            good to her

            You can see it by
            the way she gives herself
            to the one half
            sucked out in her hand

            Comforted
            a solace of ripe plums
            seeming to fill the air
            They taste good to her

Late for Summer Weather

He has on
an old light grey fedora
She a black beret

He a dirty sweater
She an old blue coat
that fits her tight

Grey flapping pants
Red skirt and
broken down black pumps

Fat Lost Ambling
nowhere through
the upper town they kick

their way through
heaps of
fallen maple leaves

still green—and
crisp as dollar bills
Nothing to do. Hot cha!

Proletarian Portrait

A big young bareheaded woman
in an apron

Her hair slicked back standing
on the street

One stockinged foot toeing
the sidewalk

Her shoe in her hand. Looking
intently into it

She pulls out the paper insole
to find the nail

That has been hurting her

Tree and Sky

Again
the bare brush of
the half-broken
and already-written-of
tree alone
on its battered
hummock—

Above
among the shufflings
of the distant
cloud-rifts
vaporously
the unmoving
blue

The Raper from Passenack

was very kind. When she regained
her wits, he said, It's all right, kid,
I took care of you.

What a mess she was in. Then he added,
You'll never forget me now.
And drove her home.

Only a man who is sick, she said
would do a thing like that.
It must be so.

No one who is not diseased could be
so insanely cruel. He wants to give it
to someone else—

to justify himself. But if I get a
venereal infection out of this
I won't be treated.

I refuse. You'll find me dead in bed
first. Why not? That's
the way she spoke,

I wish I could shoot him. How would
you like to know a murderer?
I may do it.

I'll know by the end of this week.
I wouldn't scream. I bit him
several times

but he was too strong for me.
I can't yet understand it. I don't
faint so easily.

When I came to myself and realized
what had happened all I could do
was to curse

and call him every vile name I could
think of. I was so glad
to be taken home.

I suppose it's my mind—the fear of
infection. I'd rather a million times
have been got pregnant.

But it's the foulness of it can't
be cured. And hatred, hatred of all men
—and disgust.

Invocation and Conclusion

      January!
      The beginning of all things!
      Sprung from the old burning nest
      upward in the flame!

      I was married at thirteen
      My parents had nine kids
      and we were on the street
      That's why the old bugger—

      He was twenty-six
      and I hadn't even had
      my changes yet. Now look at me!

The Yachts

contend in a sea which the land partly encloses
shielding them from the too-heavy blows
of an ungoverned ocean which when it chooses

tortures the biggest hulls, the best man knows
to pit against its beatings, and sinks them pitilessly.
Mothlike in mists, scintillant in the minute

brilliance of cloudless days, with broad bellying sails
they glide to the wind tossing green water
from their sharp prows while over them the crew crawls

ant-like, solicitously grooming them, releasing,
making fast as they turn, lean far over and having
caught the wind again, side by side, head for the mark.

In a well guarded arena of open water surrounded by
lesser and greater craft which, sycophant, lumbering
and flittering follow them, they appear youthful, rare

as the light of a happy eye, live with the grace
of all that in the mind is fleckless, free and
naturally to be desired. Now the sea which holds them

is moody, lapping their glossy sides, as if feeling
for some slightest flaw but fails completely.
Today no race. Then the wind comes again. The yachts

move, jockeying for a start, the signal is set and they
are off. Now the waves strike at them but they are too
well made, they slip through, though they take in canvas.

Arms with hands grasping seek to clutch at the prows.
Bodies thrown recklessly in the way are cut aside.
It is a sea of faces about them in agony, in despair

until the horror of the race dawns staggering the mind,
the whole sea become an entanglement of watery bodies
lost to the world bearing what they cannot hold. Broken,

beaten, desolate, reaching from the dead to be taken up
they cry out, failing, failing! their cries rising
in waves still as the skillful yachts pass over.

Hymn to Love Ended

(Imaginary translation from the Spanish)

Through what extremes of passion
had you come, Sappho, to the peace
of deathless song?

As from an illness, as after drought
the streams released to flow
filling the fields with freshness
the birds drinking from every twig
and beasts from every hollow—
bellowing, singing of the unrestraint
to colors of a waking world.
                          So
after love a music streams above it.
For what is love? But music is
Villon beaten and cast off
Shakespeare from wisdom's grotto
looking doubtful at the world
Alighieri beginning all again
Goethe whom a rose ensnared
Li Po the drunkard, singers whom
love has overthrown—

To this company the birds themselves
and the sleek beasts belong and all
who will besides—when love is ended
to the waking of sweetest song.

Sunday

Small barking sounds
Clatter of metal in a pan
A high fretting voice
and a low voice musical
as a string twanged—

The tempo is evenly drawn
give and take
A splash of water, the
ting a ring
of small pieces of metal
dropped, the clap of a door
A tune nameless as Time—

Then the voices—
Sound of feet barely moving
Slowly
And the bark, "What?"
"The same, the same, the—"
scrape of a chair
clickaty tee—

"Over Labor Day they'll
be gone"
"Jersey City, he's the
engineer—" "Ya"
"Being on the Erie R. R.
is quite convenient"

"No, I think they're—"
"I think she is. I think—"

"German-American"
"Of course the Govern—"

. . . .

A distant door slammed.
Amen.

The Catholic Bells

Tho' I'm no Catholic
I listen hard when the bells
in the yellow-brick tower
of their new church

ring down the leaves
ring in the frost upon them
and the death of the flowers
ring out the grackle

toward the south, the sky
darkened by them, ring in
the new baby of Mr. and Mrs.
Krantz which cannot

for the fat of its cheeks
open well its eyes, ring out
the parrot under its hood
jealous of the child

ring in Sunday morning
and old age which adds as it
takes away. Let them ring
only ring! over the oil

painting of a young priest
on the church wall advertising
last week's Novena to St.
Anthony, ring for the lame

young man in black with
gaunt cheeks and wearing a
Derby hat, who is hurrying
to 11 o'clock Mass (the

111

grapes still hanging to
the vine along the nearby
Concordia Halle like broken
teeth in the head of an

old man) Let them ring
for the eyes and ring for
the hands and ring for
the children of my friend

who no longer hears
them ring but with a smile
and in a low voice speaks
of the decisions of her

daughter and the proposals
and betrayals of her
husband's friends. O bells
ring for the ringing!

the beginning and the end
of the ringing! Ring ring
ring ring ring ring ring!
Catholic bells—!

The Dead Baby

Sweep the house
    under the feet of the curious
    holiday seekers--
sweep under the table and the bed
    the baby is dead--

The mother's eyes where she sits
    by the window, unconsoled--
have purple bags under them
    the father--
tall, wellspoken, pitiful
    is the abler of these two--

Sweep the house clean
    here is one who has gone up
    (though problematically)
to heaven, blindly
    by force of the facts--
a clean sweep
    is one way of expressing it--

Hurry up! any minute
    they will be bringing it
    from the hospital--
a white model of our lives
    a curiosity--
surrounded by fresh flowers

A Poem for Norman MacLeod

The revolution
is accomplished
noble has been
changed to no bull

After that
has sickered down
slumming will
be done on Park Ave.

Or as chief
One Horn said to
the constipated
prospector:

You big fool!
and with his knife
gashed a balsam
standing nearby

Gathering the
gum that oozed out
in a tin spoon
it did the trick

You can do lots
if you know
what's around you
No bull

Al Que Quiere
(To Him Who Wants it)

Sub Terra

Where shall I find you,
you my grotesque fellows
that I seek everywhere
to make up my band?
None, not one
with the earthy tastes I require;
the burrowing pride that rises
subtly as on a bush in May.

Where are you this day,
you my seven year locusts
with cased wings?
Ah my beauties how I long—!
That harvest
that shall be your advent—
thrusting up through the grass,
up under the weeds
answering me,
that will be satisfying!
The light shall leap and snap
that day as with a million lashes!

Oh, I have you; yes
you are about me in a sense:
playing under the blue pools
that are my windows,—
but they shut you out still,
there in the half light.
For the simple truth is
that though I see you clear enough
you are not there!

It is not that—it is you,
you I want!

—God, if I could fathom
the guts of shadows!

You to come with me
poking into negro houses
with their gloom and smell!
in among children
leaping around a dead dog!
Mimicking
onto the lawns of the rich!
You!
to go with me a-tip-toe,
head down under heaven,
nostrils lipping the wind!

Spring Song

Having died
one is at great advantage
over his fellows—
one can pretend.

And so,
the smell of earth
being upon you too—
I pretend

there is something
temptingly foreign
some subtle difference,
one last amour

to be divided for
our death-necklaces, when
I would merely lie
hand in hand in the dirt with you.

The Shadow

Soft as the bed in the earth
where a stone has lain—
so soft, so smooth and so cool
Spring closes me in
with her arms and her hands.

Rich as the smell
of new earth on a stone
that has lain breathing
the damp through its pores—
Spring closes me in
with her blossomy hair
brings dark to my eyes.

Pastoral

When I was younger
it was plain to me
I must make something of myself.
Older now
I walk back streets
admiring the houses
of the very poor:
roof out of line with sides
the yards cluttered
with old chicken wire, ashes,
furniture gone wrong;
the fences and outhouses
built of barrel-staves
and parts of boxes, all,
if I am fortunate,
smeared a bluish green
that properly weathered
pleases me best
of all colors.

No one
will believe this
of vast import to the nation.

Chicory and Daisies

I

Lift your flowers
on bitter stems
chicory!
Lift them up
out of the scorched ground!
Bear no foliage
but give yourself
wholly to that!
Strain under them
you bitter stems
that no beast eats—
and scorn greyness!
Into the heat with them:
cool!
luxuriant! sky-blue!
The earth cracks and
is shriveled up;
the wind moans piteously;
the sky goes out
if you should fail.

II

I saw a child with daisies
for weaving into the hair
tear the stems
with her teeth!

Metric Figure

There is a bird in the poplars!
It is the sun!
The leaves are little yellow fish
swimming in the river.
The bird skims above them,
day is on his wings.
Phoebus!
It is he that is making
the great gleam among the poplars!
It is his singing
outshines the noise
of leaves clashing in the wind.

Pastoral

The little sparrows
hop ingenuously
about the pavement
quarreling
with sharp voices
over those things
that interest them.
But we who are wiser
shut ourselves in
on either hand
and no one knows
whether we think good
or evil.

    Meanwhile,
the old man who goes about
gathering dog-lime
walks in the gutter
without looking up
and his tread
is more majestic than
that of the Episcopal minister
approaching the pulpit
of a Sunday.
    These things
astonish me beyond words.

Love Song

Daisies are broken
petals are news of the day
stems lift to the grass tops
they catch on shoes
part in the middle
leave root and leaves secure.

Black branches
carry square leaves
to the wood's top.
They hold firm
break with a roar
show the white!

Your moods are slow
the shedding of leaves
and sure
the return in May!

We walked
in your father's grove
and saw the great oaks
lying with roots
ripped from the ground.

Gulls

My townspeople, beyond in the great world,
are many with whom it were far more
profitable for me to live than here with you.
These whirr about me calling, calling!
and for my own part I answer them, loud as I can,
but they, being free, pass!
I remain! Therefore, listen!
For you will not soon have another singer.

First I say this: You have seen
the strange birds, have you not, that sometimes
rest upon our river in winter?
Let them cause you to think well then of the storms
that drive many to shelter. These things
do not happen without reason.

And the next thing I say is this:
I saw an eagle once circling against the clouds
over one of our principal churches—
Easter, it was—a beautiful day!
three gulls came from above the river
and crossed slowly seaward!
Oh, I know you have your own hymns, I have heard them—
and because I knew they invoked some great protector
I could not be angry with you, no matter
how much they outraged true music—

You see, it is not necessary for us to leap at each other,
and, as I told you, in the end
the gulls moved seaward very quietly.

Winter Sunset

Then I raised my head
and stared out over
the blue February waste
to the blue bank of hill
with stars on it
in strings and festoons—
but above that:
one opaque
stone of a cloud
just on the hill
left and right
as far as I could see;
and above that
a red streak, then
icy blue sky!

It was a fearful thing
to come into a man's heart
at that time; that stone
over the little blinking stars
they'd set there.

In Harbor

Surely there, among the great docks, is peace,
    my mind;
there with the ships moored in the river.
Go out, timid child,
and snuggle in among the great ships talking so
    quietly.
Maybe you will even fall asleep near them and be
lifted into one of their laps, and in the morning—
There is always the morning in which to remember
    it all!
Of what are they gossiping? God knows.
And God knows it matters little for we cannot
    understand them.
Yet it is certainly of the sea, of that there can be
    no question.
It is a quiet sound. Rest! That's all I care for now.
The smell of them will put us to sleep presently.
Smell! It is the sea water mingling here into the
    river—
at least so it seems—perhaps it is something else—
    but what matter?
The sea water! It is quiet and smooth here!
How slowly they move, little by little trying
the hawsers that drop and groan with their agony.
Yes, it is certainly of the high sea they are talking.

Tract

I will teach you my townspeople
how to perform a funeral
for you have it over a troop
of artists—
unless one should scour the world—
you have the ground sense necessary.

See! the hearse leads.
I begin with a design for a hearse.
For Christ's sake not black—
nor white either—and not polished!
Let it be weathered—like a farm wagon—
with gilt wheels (this could be
applied fresh at small expense)
or no wheels at all:
a rough dray to drag over the ground.

Knock the glass out!
My God—glass, my townspeople!
For what purpose? Is it for the dead
to look out or for us to see
how well he is housed or to see
the flowers or the lack of them—
or what?
To keep the rain and snow from him?
He will have a heavier rain soon:
pebbles and dirt and what not.
Let there be no glass—
and no upholstery, phew!
and no little brass rollers
and small easy wheels on the bottom—
my townspeople what are you thinking of?

A rough plain hearse then
with gilt wheels and no top at all.
On this the coffin lies
by its own weight.

                          No wreaths please—
especially no hot house flowers.
Some common memento is better,
something he prized and is known by:
his old clothes—a few books perhaps—
God knows what! You realize
how we are about these things
my townspeople—
something will be found—anything
even flowers if he had come to that.
So much for the hearse.

For heaven's sake though see to the driver!
Take off the silk hat! In fact
that's no place at all for him—
up there unceremoniously
dragging our friend out to his own dignity!
Bring him down—bring him down!
Low and inconspicuous! I'd not have him ride
on the wagon at all—damn him—
the undertaker's understrapper!
Let him hold the reins
and walk at the side
and inconspicuously too!

Then briefly as to yourselves:
Walk behind—as they do in France,
seventh class, or if you ride
Hell take curtains! Go with some show
of inconvenience; sit openly—
to the weather as to grief.

Or do you think you can shut grief in?
What—from us? We who have perhaps
nothing to lose? Share with us
share with us—it will be money
in your pockets.
                              Go now
I think you are ready.

Apology

Why do I write today?

The beauty of
the terrible faces
of our nonentities
stirs me to it:

colored women
day workers—
old and experienced—
returning home at dusk
in cast off clothing
faces like
old Florentine oak.

Also

the set pieces
of your faces stir me—
leading citizens—
but not
in the same way.

Promenade

I

Well, mind, here we have
our little son beside us:
a little diversion before breakfast!

Come, we'll walk down the road
till the bacon will be frying.
We might better be idle?
A poem might come of it?
Oh, be useful. Save annoyance
to Flossie and besides—the wind!
It's cold. It blows our
old pants out! It makes us shiver!
See the heavy trees
shifting their weight before it.
Let us be trees, an old house,
a hill with grass on it!
The baby's arms are blue.
Come, move! Be quieted!

II

So. We'll sit here now
and throw pebbles into
this water-trickle.

       Splash the water up!
(Splash it up, Sonny!) Laugh!
Hit it there deep under the grass.
See it splash! Ah, mind,
see it splash! It is alive!

Throw pieces of broken leaves
into it. They'll pass through.
No! Yes—Just!

Away now for the cows! But—
It's cold!
It's getting dark.
It's going to rain.
No further!

III

Oh, then a wreath! Let's
refresh something they
used to write well of.

Two fern plumes. Strip them
to the mid-rib along one side.
Bind the tips with a grass stem.
Bend and interwist the stalks
at the back. So!
Ah! now we are crowned!
Now we are a poet!
Quickly!
A bunch of little flowers
for Flossie—the little ones
only:

a red clover, one
blue heal-all, a sprig of
bone-set, one primrose,
a head of Indian tobacco, this
magenta speck and this
little lavender!

Home now, my mind!—
Sonny's arms are icy, I tell you—
and have breakfast!

Libertad! Igualidad! Fraternidad!

You sullen pig of a man
you force me into the mud
with your stinking ash-cart!

Brother!

                —if we were rich
we'd stick our chests out
and hold our heads high!

It is dreams that have destroyed us.

There is no more pride
in horses or in rein holding.
We sit hunched together brooding
our fate.

            Well—
all things turn bitter in the end
whether you choose the right or
the left way
                and—
dreams are not a bad thing.

Summer Song

    Wanderer moon
    smiling a
    faintly ironical smile
    at this
    brilliant, dew-moistened
    summer morning,—
    a detached
    sleepily indifferent
    smile, a
    wanderer's smile,—
    if I should
    buy a shirt
    your color and
    put on a necktie
    sky-blue
    where would they carry me?

The Young Housewife

At ten A.M. the young housewife
moves about in negligee behind
the wooden walls of her husband's house.
I pass solitary in my car.

Then again she comes to the curb
to call the ice-man, fish-man, and stands
shy, uncorseted, tucking in
stray ends of hair, and I compare her
to a fallen leaf.

The noiseless wheels of my car
rush with a crackling sound over
dried leaves as I bow and pass smiling.

Love Song

Sweep the house clean,
hang fresh curtains
in the windows
put on a new dress
and come with me!
The elm is scattering
its little loaves
of sweet smells
from a white sky!

Who shall hear of us
in the time to come?
Let him say there was
a burst of fragrance
from black branches.

Dawn

Ecstatic bird songs pound
the hollow vastness of the sky
with metallic clinkings—
beating color up into it
at a far edge,—beating it, beating it
with rising, triumphant ardor,—
stirring it into warmth,
quickening in it a spreading change,—
bursting wildly against it as
dividing the horizon, a heavy sun
lifts himself—is lifted—
bit by bit above the edge
of things,—runs free at last
out into the open—! lumbering
glorified in full release upward—
                        songs cease.

Hero

Fool,
put your adventures
into those things
which break ships—
not female flesh.

Let there pass
over the mind
the waters of
four oceans, the airs
of four skies!

Return hollow-bellied
keen-eyed, hard!
A simple scar or two.

Little girls will come
bringing you
roses for your button-hole.

Drink

My whisky is
a tough way of life:

The wild cherry
continually pressing back
peach orchards.

I am a penniless
rumsoak.

Where shall I have that solidity
which trees find
in the ground?

My stuff
is the feel of good legs
and a broad pelvis
under the gold hair ornaments
of skyscrapers.

El Hombre

It's a strange courage
you give me ancient star:

Shine alone in the sunrise
toward which you lend no part!

Winter Quiet

Limb to limb, mouth to mouth
with the bleached grass
silver mist lies upon the back yards
among the outhouses.
                    The dwarf trees
pirouette awkwardly to it—
whirling round on one toe;
the big tree smiles and glances
                              upward!
Tense with suppressed excitement
the fences watch where the ground
has humped an aching shoulder for
                        the ecstasy.

A Prelude

I know only the bare rocks of today.
In these lies my brown sea-weed,—
green quartz veins bent through the wet shale;
in these lie my pools left by the tide—
quiet, forgetting waves;
on these stiffen white star fish
on these I slip barefooted!

Whispers of the fishy air touch my body;
"Sisters," I say to them.

Trees

Crooked, black tree
on your little grey-black hillock,
ridiculously raised one step toward
the infinite summits of the night:
even you the few grey stars
draw upward into a vague melody
of harsh threads.

Bent as you are from straining
against the bitter horizontals of
a north wind,—there below you
how easily the long yellow notes
of poplars flow upward in a descending
scale, each note secure in its own
posture—singularly woven.

All voices are blent willingly
against the heaving contra-bass
of the dark but you alone
warp yourself passionately to one side
in your eagerness.

Canthara

The old black-man showed me
how he had been shocked
in his youth
by six women, dancing
a set-dance, stark naked below
the skirts raised round
their breasts:
                    bellies flung forward
knees flying!
                         —while
his gestures, against the
tiled wall of the dingy bath-room,
swished with ecstasy to
the familiar music of
                    his old emotion.

M. B.

Winter has spent this snow
out of envy, but spring is here!
He sits at the breakfast table
in his yellow hair
and disdains even the sun
walking outside
in spangled slippers:

He looks out: there is
a glare of lights
before a theater,—
a sparkling lady
passes quickly to
the seclusion of
her carriage.

     Presently
under the dirty, wavy heaven
of a borrowed room he will make
reinhaled tobacco smoke
his clouds and try them
against the sky's limits!

Good Night

In brilliant gas light
I turn the kitchen spigot
and watch the water plash
into the clean white sink.
On the grooved drain-board
to one side is
a glass filled with parsley—
crisped green.
                    Waiting
for the water to freshen—
I glance at the spotless floor—:
a pair of rubber sandals
lie side by side
under the wall-table
all is in order for the night.

Waiting, with a glass in my hand
—three girls in crimson satin
pass close before me on
the murmurous background of
the crowded opera—
                    it is
memory playing the clown—
three vague, meaningless girls
full of smells and
the rustling sounds of
cloth rubbing on cloth and
little slippers on carpet—
high-school French
spoken in a loud voice!

Parsley in a glass,
still and shining,
brings me back. I take a drink
and yawn deliciously.
I am ready for bed.

Keller Gegen Dom

Witness, would you—
one more young man
in the evening of his love
hurrying to confession:
steps down a gutter
crosses a street
goes in at a doorway
opens for you—
like some great flower—
a room filled with lamplight;
or whirls himself
obediently to
the curl of a hill
some wind-dancing afternoon;
lies for you in
the futile darkness of
a wall, sets stars dancing
to the crack of a leaf—

and—leaning his head away—
snuffs (secretly)
the bitter powder from
his thumb's hollow,
takes your blessing and
goes home to bed?

Witness instead
whether you like it or not
a dark vinegar-smelling place
from which trickles
the chuckle of
beginning laughter.

It strikes midnight.

Danse Russe

If when my wife is sleeping
and the baby and Kathleen
are sleeping
and the sun is a flame-white disc
in silken mists
above shining trees,—
if I in my north room
dance naked, grotesquely
before my mirror
waving my shirt round my head
and singing softly to myself:
"I am lonely, lonely.
I was born to be lonely,
I am best so!"
If I admire my arms, my face,
my shoulders, flanks, buttocks
against the yellow drawn shades,—

Who shall say I am not
the happy genius of my household?

Mujer

Oh, black Persian cat!
Was not your life
already cursed with offsprings?
We took you for the rest to that old
Yankee farm,—so lonely
and with so many field mice
in the long grass—
and you return to us
in this condition—!

Oh, black Persian cat.

Portrait of a Woman in Bed

There's my things
drying in the corner:
that blue skirt
joined to the grey shirt—

I'm sick of trouble!
Lift the covers
if you want me
and you'll see
the rest of my clothes—
though it would be cold
lying with nothing on!

I won't work
and I've got no cash.
What are you going to do
about it?
—and no jewelry
(the crazy fools)

But I've my two eyes
and a smooth face
and here's this! look!
it's high!

There's brains and blood
in there—
my name's Robitza!
Corsets
can go to the devil—
and drawers along with them—
What do I care!

My two boys?
—they're keen!
Let the rich lady
care for them—
they'll beat the school
or
let them go to the gutter—
that ends trouble.

This house is empty
isn't it?
Then it's mine
because I need it.
Oh, I won't starve
while there's the bible
to make them feed me.

Try to help me
if you want trouble
or leave me alone—
that ends trouble.

The country physician
is a damned fool
and you
can go to hell!

You could have closed the door
when you came in;
do it when you go out.
I'm tired.

Virtue

Now? Why—
whirlpools of
orange and purple flame
feather twists of chrome
on a green ground
funneling down upon
the steaming phallus-head
of the mad sun himself—
blackened crimson!

                              Now?

Why—
it is the smile of her
the smell of her
the vulgar inviting mouth of her
It is—Oh, nothing new
nothing that lasts
an eternity, nothing worth
putting out to interest,
nothing—
but the fixing of an eye
concretely upon emptiness!

Come! here are—
cross-eyed men, a boy
with a patch, men walking
in their shirts, men in hats
dark men, a pale man
with little black moustaches
and a dirty white coat,
fat men with pudgy faces,
thin faces, crooked faces
slit eyes, grey eyes, black eyes

old men with dirty beards,
men in vests with
gold watch chains. Come!

Smell!

Oh strong-ridged and deeply hollowed
nose of mine! what will you not be smelling?
What tactless asses we are, you and I boney nose
always indiscriminate, always unashamed,
and now it is the souring flowers of the bedraggled
poplars: a festering pulp on the wet earth
beneath them. With what deep thirst
we quicken our desires
to that rank odor of a passing springtime!
Can you not be decent? Can you not reserve your ardors
for something less unlovely? What girl will care
for us, do you think, if we continue in these ways?
Must you taste everything? Must you know everything?
Must you have a part in everything?

The Ogre

Sweet child,
little girl with well-shaped legs
you cannot touch the thoughts
I put over and under and around you.
This is fortunate for they would
burn you to an ash otherwise.
Your petals would be quite curled up.

This is all beyond you—no doubt,
yet you do feel the brushings
of the fine needles;
the tentative lines of your whole body
prove it to me;
so does your fear of me,
your shyness;
likewise the toy baby cart
that you are pushing—
and besides, mother has begun
to dress your hair in a knot.
These are my excuses.

Sympathetic Portrait of a Child

The murderer's little daughter
who is barely ten years old
jerks her shoulders
right and left
so as to catch a glimpse of me
without turning round.

Her skinny little arms
wrap themselves
this way then that
reversely about her body!
Nervously
she crushes her straw hat
about her eyes
and tilts her head
to deepen the shadow—
smiling excitedly!

As best she can
she hides herself
in the full sunlight
her cordy legs writhing
beneath the little flowered dress
that leaves them bare
from mid-thigh to ankle—

Why has she chosen me
for the knife
that darts along her smile?

Riposte

Love is like water or the air
my townspeople;
it cleanses, and dissipates evil gases.
It is like poetry too
and for the same reasons.

Love is so precious
my townspeople
that if I were you I would
have it under lock and key—
like the air or the Atlantic or
like poetry!

K. McB.

You exquisite chunk of mud
Kathleen—just like
any other chunk of mud!
—especially April!
Curl up round their shoes
when they try to step on you,
spoil the polish!
I shall laugh till I am sick
at their amazement.
Do they expect the ground to be
always solid?
Give them the slip then;
let them sit in you;
soil their pants;
teach them a dignity
that is dignity, the dignity
of mud!

        Lie basking in
the sun then—fast asleep!
Even become dust on occasion.

The Old Men

Old men who have studied
every leg show
in the city
Old men cut from touch
by the perfumed music—
polished or fleeced skulls
that stand before
the whole theater
in silent attitudes
of attention,—
old men who have taken precedence
over young men
and even over dark-faced
husbands whose minds
are a street with arc-lights.
Solitary old men for whom
we find no excuses—
I bow my head in shame
for those who malign you.
Old men
the peaceful beer of impotence
be yours!

Spring Strains

In a tissue-thin monotone of blue-grey buds
crowded erect with desire against the sky
      tense blue-grey twigs
slenderly anchoring them down, drawing
them in—

      two blue-grey birds chasing
a third struggle in circles, angles,
swift convergings to a point that bursts
instantly!

      Vibrant bowing limbs
pull downward, sucking in the sky
that bulges from behind, plastering itself
against them in packed rifts, rock blue
and dirty orange!

                  But—
(Hold hard, rigid jointed trees!)
the blinding and red-edged sun-blur—
creeping energy, concentrated
counterforce—welds sky, buds, trees,
rivets them in one puckering hold!
Sticks through! Pulls the whole
counter-pulling mass upward, to the right
locks even the opaque, not yet defined
ground in a terrific drag that is
loosening the very tap-roots!

On a tissue-thin monotone of blue-grey buds
two blue-grey birds, chasing a third,
at full cry! Now they are
flung outward and up—disappearing suddenly!

159

A Portrait in Greys

Will it never be possible
to separate you from your greyness?
Must you be always sinking backwards
into your grey-brown landscapes—and trees
always in the distance, always against
a grey sky?
       Must I be always
moving counter to you? Is there no place
where we can be at peace together
and the motion of our drawing apart
be altogether taken up?
       I see myself
standing upon your shoulders touching
a grey, broken sky—
but you, weighted down with me,
yet gripping my ankles,—move
       laboriously on,
where it is level and undisturbed by colors.

Pastoral

If I say I have heard voices
who will believe me?

"None has dipped his hand
in the black waters of the sky
nor picked the yellow lilies
that sway on their clear stems
and no tree has waited
long enough nor still enough
to touch fingers with the moon."

I looked and there were little frogs
with puffed-out throats,
singing in the slime.

January Morning

I

I have discovered that most of
the beauties of travel are due to
the strange hours we keep to see them:

the domes of the Church of
the Paulist Fathers in Weehawken
against a smoky dawn—the heart stirred—
are beautiful as Saint Peters
approached after years of anticipation.

II

Though the operation was postponed
I saw the tall probationers
in their tan uniforms
                        hurrying to breakfast!

III

—and from basement entries
neatly coiffed, middle aged gentlemen
with orderly moustaches and
well-brushed coats

IV

—and the sun, dipping into the avenues
streaking the tops of

the irregular red houselets,
                              and
the gay shadows dropping and dropping.

                    V

—and a young horse with a green bed-quilt
on his withers shaking his head:
bared teeth and nozzle high in the air!

                    VI

—and a semicircle of dirt-colored men
about a fire bursting from an old
ash can,

                    VII

            —and the worn,
blue car rails (like the sky!)
gleaming among the cobbles!

                    VIII

—and the rickety ferry-boat "Arden"!
What an object to be called "Arden"
among the great piers,—on the
ever new river!
            "Put me a Touchstone
at the wheel, white gulls, and we'll
follow the ghost of the *Half Moon*
to the North West Passage—and through!
(at Albany!) for all that!"

163

IX

Exquisite brown waves—long
circlets of silver moving over you!
enough with crumbling ice crusts among you!
The sky has come down to you,
lighter than tiny bubbles, face to
face with you!
                                His spirit is
a white gull with delicate pink feet
and a snowy breast for you to
hold to your lips delicately!

X

The young doctor is dancing with happiness
in the sparkling wind, alone
at the prow of the ferry! He notices
the curdy barnacles and broken ice crusts
left at the slip's base by the low tide
and thinks of summer and green
shell-crusted ledges among
                                the emerald eel-grass!

XI

Who knows the Palisades as I do
knows the river breaks east from them
above the city—but they continue south
—under the sky—to bear a crest of
little peering houses that brighten
with dawn behind the moody
water-loving giants of Manhattan.

Long yellow rushes bending
above the white snow patches;
purple and gold ribbon
of the distant wood:
          what an angle
you make with each other as
you lie there in contemplation.

XIII

Work hard all your young days
and they'll find you too, some morning
staring up under
your chiffonier at its warped
bass-wood bottom and your soul—
out!
—among the little sparrows
behind the shutter.

XIV

—and the flapping flags are at
half mast for the dead admiral.

XV

All this—
          was for you, old woman.
I wanted to write a poem
that you would understand.
For what good is it to me

if you can't understand it?
               But you got to try hard—
But—
      Well, you know how
the young girls run giggling
on Park Avenue after dark
when they ought to be home in bed?
Well,
that's the way it is with me somehow.

To a Solitary Disciple

Rather notice, mon cher,
that the moon is
tilted above
the point of the steeple
than that its color
is shell-pink.

Rather observe
that it is early morning
than that the sky
is smooth
as a turquoise.

Rather grasp
how the dark
converging lines
of the steeple
meet at the pinnacle—
perceive how
its little ornament
tries to stop them—

See how it fails!
See how the converging lines
of the hexagonal spire
escape upward—
receding, dividing!
—sepals
that guard and contain
the flower!

Observe
how motionless

the eaten moon
lies in the protecting lines.
It is true:
in the light colors
of morning

brown-stone and slate
shine orange and dark blue.

But observe
the oppressive weight
of the squat edifice!
Observe
the jasmine lightness
of the moon.

Ballet

Are you not weary,
great gold cross
shining in the wind—
are you not weary
of seeing the stars
turning over you
and the sun
going to his rest
and you frozen with
a great lie
that leaves you
rigid as a knight
on a marble coffin?

—and you?
higher, still,
          robin,
untwisting a song
from the bare
top-twigs,
are you not
weary of labor,
even the labor of
a song?
Come down—join me
for I am lonely.

First it will be
a quiet pace
to ease our stiffness
but as the west yellows
you will be ready!
Here in the middle

of the roadway
we will fling
ourselves round
with dust lilies
till we are bound in
their twining stems!
We will tear
their flowers
with arms flashing!

And when
the astonished stars
push aside
their curtains
they will see us
fall exhausted where
wheels and
the pounding feet
of horses
will crush forth
our laughter.

Dedication for a Plot of Ground

This plot of ground
facing the waters of this inlet
is dedicated to the living presence of
Emily Dickinson Wellcome
who was born in England, married,
lost her husband and with
her five year old son
sailed for New York in a two-master,
was driven to the Azores;
ran adrift on Fire Island shoal,
met her second husband
in a Brooklyn boarding house,
went with him to Puerto Rico
bore three more children, lost
her second husband, lived hard
for eight years in St. Thomas,
Puerto Rico, San Domingo, followed
the oldest son to New York,
lost her daughter, lost her "baby",
seized the two boys of
the oldest son by the second marriage
mothered them—they being
motherless—fought for them
against the other grandmother
and the aunts, brought them here
summer after summer, defended
herself here against thieves,
storms, sun, fire,
against flies, against girls
that came smelling about, against
drought, against weeds, storm-tides,
neighbors, weasels that stole her chickens,
against the weakness of her own hands,

against the growing strength of
the boys, against wind, against
the stones, against trespassers,
against rents, against her own mind.

She grubbed this earth with her own hands,
domineered over this grass plot,
blackguarded her oldest son
into buying it, lived here fifteen years,
attained a final loneliness and—

If you can bring nothing to this place
but your carcass, keep out.

Conquest

(Dedicated to F. W.)

Hard, chilly colors:
straw-grey, frost-grey
the grey of frozen ground:
and you, O Sun,
close above the horizon!
It is I holds you—
half against the sky
half against a black tree trunk
icily resplendent!

Lie there, blue city, mine at last—
rimming the banked blue-grey
and rise, indescribable smoky-yellow
into the overpowering white!

What have I to say to you
When we shall meet?
Yet—
I lie here thinking of you.

The stain of love
Is upon the world.
Yellow, yellow, yellow,
It eats into the leaves,
Smears with saffron
The horned branches that lean
Heavily
Against a smooth purple sky.

There is no light—
Only a honey-thick stain
That drips from leaf to leaf
And limb to limb
Spoiling the colors
Of the whole world.

I am alone.
The weight of love
Has buoyed me up
Till my head
Knocks against the sky.

See me!
My hair is dripping with nectar—
Starlings carry it
On their black wings.
See at last
My arms and my hands
Are lying idle.

How can I tell
If I shall ever love you again
As I do now?

Love Song

I lie here thinking of you:—

the stain of love
is upon the world!
Yellow, yellow, yellow
it eats into the leaves,
smears with saffron
the horned branches that lean
heavily
against a smooth purple sky!
There is no light
only a honey-thick stain
that drips from leaf to leaf
and limb to limb
spoiling the colors
of the whole world—

you far off there under
the wine-red selvage of the west!

Fish

•

Romance Moderne

Fish

It is the whales that drive
the small fish into the fiords.
I have seen forty or fifty
of them in the water at one time.
I have been in a little boat
when the water was boiling
on all sides of us
from them swimming underneath.

The noise of the herring
can be heard nearly a mile.
So thick in the water, they are,
you can't dip the oars in.
All silver!

And all those millions of fish
must be taken, each one, by hand.
The women and children
pull out a little piece
under the throat with their fingers
so that the brine gets inside.

I have seen thousands of barrels
packed with the fish on the shore.

In winter they set the gill-nets
for the cod. Hundreds of them
are caught each night.
In the morning the men
pull in the nets and fish
altogether in the boats.
Cod so big—I have seen—
that when a man held one up

above his head
the tail swept the ground.

Sardines, mackerel, anchovies
all of these. And in the rivers
trout and salmon. I have seen
a net set at the foot of a falls
and in the morning sixty trout in it.

But I guess there are not
such fish in Norway nowadays.

On the Lofoten Islands—
till I was twelve.
Not a tree or a shrub on them.
But in summer
with the sun never gone
the grass is higher than here.

The sun circles the horizon.
Between twelve and one at night
it is very low, near the sea,
to the north. Then
it rises a little, slowly,
till midday, then down again
and so for three months, getting
higher at first, then lower,
until it disappears—

In winter the snow is often
as deep as the ceiling of this room.

If you go there you will see
many Englishmen
near the falls and on the bridges
fishing, fishing.

They will stand there for hours
to catch the fish.

Near the shore
where the water is twenty feet or so
you can see the kingflounders
on the sand. They have
red spots on the side. Men come
in boats and stick them
with long pointed poles.

Have you seen how the Swedes drink tea?
So, in the saucer. They blow it
and turn it this way then that: so.

Tall, gaunt
great drooping nose, eyes dark-circled,
the voice slow and smiling:

I have seen boys stand
where the stream is narrow
a foot each side on two rocks
and grip the trout as they pass through.
They have a special way to hold them,
in the gills, so. The long
fingers arched like grapplehooks.

Then the impatient silence
while a little man said:

The English are great sportsmen.
At the winter resorts
where I stayed
they were always the first up
in the morning, the first

on with the skis.
I once saw a young Englishman
worth seventy million pounds—

You do not know the north.
—and you will see perhaps *huldra*
with long tails
and all blue, from the night,
and the *nekke*, half man and half fish.
When they see one of them
they know some boat will be lost.

Romance Moderne

Tracks of rain and light linger in
the spongy greens of a nature whose
flickering mountain—bulging nearer,
ebbing back into the sun
hollowing itself away to hold a lake,—
or brown stream rising and falling
at the roadside, turning about,
churning itself white, drawing
green in over it,—plunging glassy funnels
fall—

    And—the other world—
the windshield a blunt barrier:
Talk to me. Sh! they would hear us.
—the backs of their heads facing us—
The stream continues its motion of
a hound running over rough ground.

Trees vanish—reappear—vanish:
detached dance of gnomes—as a talk
dodging remarks, glows and fades.
—The unseen power of words—
And now that a few of the moves
are clear the first desire is
to fling oneself out at the side into
the other dance, to other music.

Peer Gynt. Rip Van Winkle. Diana.
If I were young I would try a new alignment—
alight nimbly from the car, Good-bye!—
Childhood companions linked two and two
criss-cross: four, three, two, one.
Back into self, tentacles withdrawn.

Feel about in warm self-flesh.
Since childhood, since childhood!
Childhood is a toad in the garden, a
happy toad. All toads are happy
and belong in gardens. A toad to Diana!

Lean forward. Punch the steersman
behind the ear. Twirl the wheel!
Over the edge! Screams! Crash!
The end. I sit above my head—
a little removed—or
a thin wash of rain on the roadway
—I am never afraid when he is driving,—
interposes new direction,
rides us sidewise, unforseen
into the ditch! All threads cut!
Death! Black. The end. The very end—

I would sit separate weighing a
small red handful: the dirt of these parts,
sliding mists sheeting the alders
against the touch of fingers creeping
to mine. All stuff of the blind emotions.
But—stirred, the eye seizes
for the first time—The eye awake!—
anything, a dirt bank with green stars
of scrawny weed flattened upon it under
a weight of air—For the first time!—
or a yawning depth: Big!
Swim around in it, through it—
all directions and find
vitreous seawater stuff—
God how I love you!—or, as I say,
a plunge into the ditch. The end. I sit
examining my red handful. Balancing
—this—in and out—agh.

Love you? It's
a fire in the blood, willy-nilly!
It's the sun coming up in the morning.
Ha, but it's the grey moon too, already up
in the morning. You are slow.
Men are not friends where it concerns
a woman. Fighters. Playfellows.
White round thighs! Youth! Sighs—!
It's the fillip of novelty. It's—

Mountains. Elephants humping along
against the sky—indifferent to
light withdrawing its tattered shreds,
worn out with embraces. It's
the fillip of novelty. It's a fire in the blood.

Oh, get a flannel shirt, white flannel
or pongee. You'd look so well!
I married you because I liked your nose.
I wanted you! I wanted you
in spite of all they'd say—

Rain and light, mountain and rain,
rain and river. Will you love me always?
—A car overturned and two crushed bodies
under it.—Always! Always!
And the white moon already up.
White. Clean. All the colors.
A good head, backed by the eye—awake!
backed by the emotions—blind—
River and mountain, light and rain—or
rain, rock, light, trees—divided:
rain-light counter rocks—trees or
trees counter rain-light-rocks or—

Myriads of counter processions

crossing and recrossing, regaining
the advantage, buying here, selling there
—You are sold cheap everywhere in town!—
lingering, touching fingers, withdrawing
gathering forces into blares, hummocks,
peaks and rivers—river meeting rock
—I wish that you were lying there dead
and I sitting here beside you.—
It's the grey moon—over and over.
It's the clay of these parts.

Sour Grapes

The Late Singer

Here it is spring again
and I still a young man!
I am late at my singing.
The sparrow with the black rain on his breast
has been at his cadenzas for two weeks past:
What is it that is dragging at my heart?
The grass by the back door
is stiff with sap.
The old maples are opening
their branches of brown and yellow moth-flowers.
A moon hangs in the blue
in the early afternoons over the marshes.
I am late at my singing.

A Celebration

A middle-northern March, now as always—
gusts from the South broken against cold winds—
but from under, as if a slow hand lifted a tide,
it moves—not into April—into a second March,

the old skin of wind-clear scales dropping
upon the mold: this is the shadow projects the tree
upward causing the sun to shine in his sphere.

So we will put on our pink felt hat—new last year!
—newer this by virtue of brown eyes turning back
the seasons—and let us walk to the orchid-house,
see the flowers will take the prize tomorrow
at the Palace.
                    Stop here, these are our oleanders.
When they are in bloom—
                              You would waste words
It is clearer to me than if the pink
were on the branch. It would be a searching in
a colored cloud to reveal that which now, huskless,
shows the very reason for their being.

And these the orange-trees, in blossom—no need
to tell with this weight of perfume in the air.
If it were not so dark in this shed one could better
see the white.
                    It is that very perfume
has drawn the darkness down among the leaves.
Do I speak clearly enough?
It is this darkness reveals that which darkness alone
loosens and sets spinning on waxen wings—
not the touch of a finger-tip, not the motion
of a sigh. A too heavy sweetness proves
188

its own caretaker.
And here are the orchids!
                    Never having seen
such gaiety I will read these flowers for you:
This is an old January, died—in Villon's time.
Snow, this is and this the stain of violet
grew in that place the spring that foresaw its own doom.

And this, a certain July from Iceland:
a young woman of that place
breathed it toward the South. It took root there.
The color ran true but the plant is small.

This falling spray of snow-flakes is
a handful of dead Februaries
prayed into flower by Rafael Arevalo Martinez
of Guatemala.
                    Here's that old friend who
went by my side for so many years, this full, fragile
head of veined lavender. Oh that April
that we first went with our stiff lusts
leaving the city behind, out to the green hill—
May, they said she was. A hand for all of us:
this branch of blue butterflies tied to this stem.

June is a yellow cup I'll not name; August
the over-heavy one. And here are—
russet and shiny, all but March. And March?
Ah, March—
                    Flowers are a tiresome pastime.
One has a wish to shake them from their pots
root and stem, for the sun to gnaw.

Walk out again into the cold and saunter home
to the fire. This day has blossomed long enough.
I have wiped out the red night and lit a blaze

instead which will at least warm our hands
and stir up the talk.

        I think we have kept fair time.
Time is a green orchid.

April

If you had come away with me
into another state
we had been quiet together.
But there the sun coming up
out of the nothing beyond the lake was
too low in the sky,
there was too great a pushing
against him,
too much of sumac buds, pink
in the head
with the clear gum upon them,
too many opening hearts of lilac leaves,
too many, too many swollen
limp poplar tassels on the
bare branches!
It was too strong in the air.
I had no rest against that
springtime!
The pounding of the hoofs on the
raw sods
stayed with me half through the night.
I awoke smiling but tired.

At Night

The stars, that are small lights—
now that I know them foreign,
uninterfering, like nothing
in my life—I walk by their sparkle
relieved and comforted. Or when
the moon moves slowly up among them
with flat shine then the night
has a novel light in it—curved
curiously in a thin half-circle

Berket and the Stars

A day on the boulevards chosen out of ten years of
student poverty! One best day out of ten good ones.
Berket in high spirits—"Ha, oranges! Let's have one!"
And he made to snatch an orange from a vendor's cart.

Now so clever was the deception, so nicely timed
to the full sweep of certain wave summits,
that the rumor of the thing has come down through
three generations—which is relatively forever!

A Good Night

Go to sleep—though of course you will not—
to tideless waves thundering slantwise against
strong embankments, rattle and swish of spray
dashed thirty feet high, caught by the lake wind,
scattered and strewn broadcast in over the steady
car rails! Sleep, sleep! Gulls' cries in a wind-gust
broken by the wind; calculating wings set above
the field of waves breaking.
Go to sleep to the lunge between foam-crests,
refuse churned in the recoil. Food! Food!
Offal! Offal! that holds them in the air, wave-white
for the one purpose, feather upon feather, the wild
chill in their eyes, the hoarseness in their voices—
sleep, sleep . . .

Gentlefooted crowds are treading out your lullaby.
Their arms nudge, they brush shoulders,
hitch this way then that, mass and surge at the crossings—
lullaby, lullaby! The wild-fowl police whistles,
the enraged roar of the traffic, machine shrieks:
it is all to put you to sleep,
to soften your limbs in relaxed postures,
and that your head slip sidewise, and your hair loosen
and fall over your eyes and over your mouth,
brushing your lips wistfully that you may dream,
sleep and dream—

A black fungus springs out about lonely church doors—
sleep, sleep. The night, coming down upon
the wet boulevard, would start you awake with his
message, to have in at your window. Pay no
heed to him. He storms at your sill with
cooings, with gesticulations, curses!
You will not let him in. He would keep you from sleeping.

192

He would have you sit under your desk lamp
brooding, pondering; he would have you
slide out the drawer, take up the ornamented dagger
and handle it. It is late, it is nineteen-nineteen—
go to sleep, his cries are a lullaby;
his jabbering is a sleep-well-my-baby; he is
a crackbrained messenger.

The maid waking you in the morning
when you are up and dressing
the rustle of your clothes as you raise them—
it is the same tune.
At the table the cold, greenish, split grapefruit, its juice
on the tongue, the clink of the spoon in
your coffee, the toast odors say it over and over.

The open street-door lets in the breath of
the morning wind from over the lake.
The bus coming to a halt grinds from its sullen brakes—
lullaby, lullaby. The crackle of a newspaper,
the movement of the troubled coat beside you—
sleep, sleep, sleep, sleep . . .
It is the sting of snow, the burning liquor of
the moonlight, the rush of rain in the gutters packed
with dead leaves: go to sleep, go to sleep.
And the night passes—and never passes—

Overture to a Dance of Locomotives

I

Men with picked voices chant the names
of cities in a huge gallery: promises
that pull through descending stairways
to a deep rumbling.

                 The rubbing feet
of those coming to be carried quicken a
grey pavement into soft light that rocks
to and fro, under the domed ceiling,
across and across from pale
earthcolored walls of bare limestone.

Covertly the hands of a great clock
go round and round! Were they to
move quickly and at once the whole
secret would be out and the shuffling
of all ants be done forever.

A leaning pyramid of sunlight, narrowing
out at a high window, moves by the clock;
discordant hands straining out from
a center: inevitable postures infinitely
repeated—

two—twofour—twoeight!

Porters in red hats run on narrow platforms.

This way ma'am!
                —important not to take
the wrong train!

            Lights from the concrete
ceiling hang crooked but—
                    Poised horizontal
on glittering parallels the dingy cylinders
packed with a warm glow—inviting entry—
pull against the hour. But brakes can
hold a fixed posture till—
                    The whistle!

Not twoeight. Not twofour. Two!

Gliding windows. Colored cooks sweating
in a small kitchen. Taillights—
In time: twofour!
In time: twoeight!

—rivers are tunneled: trestles
cross oozy swampland: wheels repeating
the same gesture remain relatively
stationary: rails forever parallel
return on themselves infinitely.
                    The dance is sure.

The Desolate Field

Vast and grey, the sky
is a simulacrum
to all but him whose days
are vast and grey, and—
In the tall, dried grasses
a goat stirs
with nozzle searching the ground.
—my head is in the air
but who am I . . ?
And amazed my heart leaps
at the thought of love
vast and grey
yearning silently over me.

Willow Poem

It is a willow when summer is over,
a willow by the river
from which no leaf has fallen nor
bitten by the sun
turned orange or crimson.
The leaves cling and grow paler,
swing and grow paler
over the swirling waters of the river
as if loath to let go,
they are so cool, so drunk with
the swirl of the wind and of the river—
oblivious to winter,
the last to let go and fall
into the water and on the ground.

Approach of Winter

The half-stripped trees
struck by a wind together,
bending all,
the leaves flutter drily
and refuse to let go
or driven like hail
stream bitterly out to one side
and fall
where the salvias, hard carmine,—
like no leaf that ever was—
edge the bare garden.

January

Again I reply to the triple winds
running chromatic fifths of derision
outside my window:
                    Play louder.
You will not succeed. I am
bound more to my sentences
the more you batter at me
to follow you.
                    And the wind,
as before, fingers perfectly
its derisive music.

Blizzard

Snow:
years of anger following
hours that float idly down—
the blizzard
drifts its weight
deeper and deeper for three days
or sixty years, eh? Then
the sun! a clutter of
yellow and blue flakes—
Hairy looking trees stand out
in long alleys
over a wild solitude.
The man turns and there—
his solitary tracks stretched out
upon the world.

Complaint

They call me and I go.
It is a frozen road
past midnight, a dust
of snow caught
in the rigid wheeltracks.
The door opens.
I smile, enter and
shake off the cold.
Here is a great woman
on her side in the bed.
She is sick,
perhaps vomiting,
perhaps laboring
to give birth to
a tenth child. Joy! Joy!
Night is a room
darkened for lovers,
through the jalousies the sun
has sent one gold needle!
I pick the hair from her eyes
and watch her misery
with compassion.

To Waken An Old Lady

Old age is
a flight of small
cheeping birds
skimming
bare trees
above a snow glaze.
Gaining and failing
they are buffeted
by a dark wind—
But what?
On harsh weedstalks
the flock has rested,
the snow
is covered with broken
seedhusks
and the wind tempered
by a shrill
piping of plenty.

Winter Trees

All the complicated details
of the attiring and
the disattiring are completed!
A liquid moon
moves gently among
the long branches.
Thus having prepared their buds
against a sure winter
the wise trees
stand sleeping in the cold.

The Dark Day

A three-day-long rain from the east—
an interminable talking, talking
of no consequence—patter, patter, patter.
Hand in hand little winds
blow the thin streams aslant.
Warm. Distance cut off. Seclusion.
A few passers-by, drawn in upon themselves,
hurry from one place to another.
Winds of the white poppy! there is no escape!—
An interminable talking, talking,
talking . . . it has happened before.
Backward, backward, backward.

Spring Storm

The sky has given over
its bitterness.
Out of the dark change
all day long
rain falls and falls
as if it would never end.
Still the snow keeps
its hold on the ground.
But water, water
from a thousand runnels!
It collects swiftly,
dappled with black
cuts a way for itself
through green ice in the gutters.
Drop after drop it falls
from the withered grass-stems
of the overhanging embankment.

Thursday

I have had my dream—like others—
and it has come to nothing, so that
I remain now carelessly
with feet planted on the ground
and look up at the sky—
feeling my clothes about me,
the weight of my body in my shoes,
the rim of my hat, air passing in and out
at my nose—and decide to dream no more.

The Cold Night

It is cold. The white moon
is up among her scattered stars—
like the bare thighs of
the Police Sergeant's wife—among
her five children . . .
No answer. Pale shadows lie upon
the frosted grass. One answer:
It is midnight, it is still
and it is cold . . . !
White thighs of the sky! a
new answer out of the depths of
my male belly: In April . . .
In April I shall see again—In April!
the round and perfect thighs
of the Police Sergeant's wife
perfect still after many babies.
Oya!

To Be Closely Written On A Small Piece Of Paper Which Folded Into A Tight Lozenge Will Fit Any Girl's Locket

Lo the leaves
Upon the new autumn grass—
Look at them well . !

The Young Laundryman

Ladies, I crave your indulgence for
My friend Wu Kee; young, agile, clear-eyed
And clean-limbed, his muscles ripple
Under the thin blue shirt; and his naked feet, in
Their straw sandals, lift at the heels, shift and
Find new postures continually.

Your husband's shirts to wash, please, for Wu Kee.

Time The Hangman

Poor old Abner, poor old white-haired nigger!
I remember when you were so strong
you hung yourself by a rope round the neck
in Doc Hollister's barn to prove you could beat
the faker in the circus—and it didn't kill you.
Now your face is in your hands, and your elbows
are on your knees, and you are silent and broken.

204

To a Friend

Well, Lizzie Anderson! seventeen men—and
the baby hard to find a father for!

What will the good Father in Heaven say
to the local judge if he do not solve this problem?
A little two-pointed smile and—pouff!—
the law is changed into a mouthful of phrases.

The Gentle Man

I feel the caress of my own fingers
on my own neck as I place my collar
and think pityingly
of the kind women I have known.

The Soughing Wind

Some leaves hang late, some fall
before the first frost—so goes
the tale of winter branches and old bones.

Spring

O my grey hairs!
You are truly white as plum blossoms.

Play

Subtle, clever brain, wiser than I am,
by what devious means do you contrive
to remain idle? Teach me, O master.

Lines

Leaves are grey green,
the glass broken, bright green.

The Poor

By constantly tormenting them
with reminders of the lice in
their children's hair, the
School Physician first
brought their hatred down on him.
But by this familiarity
they grew used to him, and so,
at last,
took him for their friend and adviser.

Complete Destruction

> It was an icy day,
> We buried the cat,
> then took her box
> and set match to it
>
> in the back yard.
> Those fleas that escaped
> earth and fire
> died by the cold.

Memory of April

> You say love is this, love is that:
> Poplar tassels, willow tendrils
> the wind and the rain comb,
> tinkle and drip, tinkle and drip—
> branches drifting apart. Hagh!
> Love has not even visited this country.

Daisy

The dayseye hugging the earth
in August, ha! Spring is
gone down in purple,
weeds stand high in the corn,
the rainbeaten furrow
is clotted with sorrel
and crabgrass, the
branch is black under
the heavy mass of the leaves—
The sun is upon a
slender green stem
ribbed lengthwise.
He lies on his back—
it is a woman also—
he regards his former
majesty and
round the yellow center,
split and creviced and done into
minute flowerheads, he sends out
his twenty rays—a little
and the wind is among them
to grow cool there!

One turns the thing over
in his hand and looks
at it from the rear: brownedged,
green and pointed scales
armor his yellow.

But turn and turn,
the crisp petals remain
brief, translucent, greenfastened,
barely touching at the edges:
blades of limpid seashell.

Primrose

Yellow, yellow, yellow, yellow!
It is not a color.
It is summer!
It is the wind on a willow,
the lap of waves, the shadow
under a bush, a bird, a bluebird,
three herons, a dead hawk
rotting on a pole—
Clear yellow!
It is a piece of blue paper
in the grass or a threecluster of
green walnuts swaying, children
playing croquet or one boy
fishing, a man
swinging his pink fists
as he walks—
It is ladysthumb, forget-me-nots
in the ditch, moss under
the flange of the carrail, the
wavy lines in split rock, a
great oaktree—
It is a disinclination to be
five red petals or a rose, it is
a cluster of birdsbreast flowers
on a red stem six feet high,
four open yellow petals
above sepals curled
backward into reverse spikes—
Tufts of purple grass spot the
green meadow and clouds the sky.

Queen-Ann's-Lace

Her body is not so white as
anemone petals nor so smooth—nor
so remote a thing. It is a field
of the wild carrot taking
the field by force; the grass
does not raise above it.
Here is no question of whiteness,
white as can be, with a purple mole
at the center of each flower.
Each flower is a hand's span
of her whiteness. Wherever
his hand has lain there is
a tiny purple blemish. Each part
is a blossom under his touch
to which the fibres of her being
stem one by one, each to its end,
until the whole field is a
white desire, empty, a single stem,
a cluster, flower by flower,
a pious wish to whiteness gone over—
or nothing.

Great Mullen

One leaves his leaves at home
being a mullen and sends up a lighthouse
to peer from: I will have my way,
yellow—A mast with a lantern, ten
fifty, a hundred, smaller and smaller
as they grow more—Liar, liar, liar!
You come from her! I can smell djer-kiss
on your clothes. Ha! you come to me,
you—I am a point of dew on a grass-stem.
Why are you sending heat down on me
from your lantern?—You are cowdung, a
dead stick with the bark off. She is
squirting on us both. She has had her
hand on you!—well?—She has defiled
ME.—Your leaves are dull, thick
and hairy.—Every hair on my body will
hold you off from me. You are a
dungcake, birdlime on a fencerail.—
I love you, straight, yellow
finger of God pointing to—her!
Liar, broken weed, dungcake, you have—
I am a cricket waving his antennae
and you are high, grey and straight. Ha!

Epitaph

An old willow with hollow branches
slowly swayed his few high bright tendrils
and sang:

Love is a young green willow
shimmering at the bare wood's edge.

Waiting

When I am alone I am happy.
The air is cool. The sky is
flecked and splashed and wound
with color. The crimson phalloi
of the sassafras leaves
hang crowded before me
in shoals on the heavy branches.
When I reach my doorstep
I am greeted by
the happy shrieks of my children
and my heart sinks.
I am crushed.

Are not my children as dear to me
as falling leaves or
must one become stupid
to grow older?
It seems much as if Sorrow
had tripped up my heels.
Let us see, let us see!
What did I plan to say to her
when it should happen to me
as it has happened now?

The Hunter

In the flashes and black shadows
of July
the days, locked in each other's arms,
seem still
so that squirrels and colored birds
go about at ease over
the branches and through the air.

Where will a shoulder split or
a forehead open and victory be?

Nowhere.
Both sides grow older.

And you may be sure
not one leaf will lift itself
from the ground
and become fast to a twig again.

Arrival

And yet one arrives somehow,
finds himself loosening the hooks of
her dress
in a strange bedroom—
feels the autumn
dropping its silk and linen leaves
about her ankles.
The tawdry veined body emerges
twisted upon itself
like a winter wind . . . !

To a Friend Concerning Several Ladies

You know there is not much
that I desire, a few chrysanthemums
half lying on the grass, yellow
and brown and white, the
talk of a few people, the trees,
an expanse of dried leaves perhaps
with ditches among them.

But there comes
between me and these things
a letter
or even a look—well placed,
you understand,
so that I am confused, twisted
four ways and—left flat,
unable to lift the food to
my own mouth:
Here is what they say: Come!
and come! and come! And if
I do not go I remain stale to
myself and if I go—
                    I have watched
the city from a distance at night
and wondered why I wrote no poem.
Come! yes,
the city is ablaze for you
and you stand and look at it.

And they are right. There is
no good in the world except out of
a woman and certain women alone
for certain things. But what if
I arrive like a turtle,

with my house on my back or
a fish ogling from under water?
It will not do. I must be
steaming with love, colored
like a flamingo. For what?
To have legs and a silly head
and to smell, pah! like a flamingo
that soils its own feathers behind?
Must I go home filled
with a bad poem?
And they say:
Who can answer these things
till he has tried? Your eyes
are half closed, you are a child,
oh, a sweet one, ready to play
but I will make a man of you and
with love on his shoulder—!

And in the marshes
the crickets run
on the sunny dike's top and
make burrows there, the water
reflects the reeds and the reeds
move on their stalks and rattle drily.

The Disputants

Upon the table in their bowl!
in violent disarray
of yellow sprays, green spikes
of leaves, red pointed petals
and curled heads of blue
and white among the litter
of the forks and crumbs and plates
the flowers remain composed.
Coolly their colloquy continues
above the coffee and loud talk
grown frail as vaudeville.

The Birds

The world begins again!
Not wholly insufflated
the blackbirds in the rain
upon the dead topbranches
of the living tree,
stuck fast to the low clouds,
notate the dawn.
Their shrill cries sound
announcing appetite
and drop among the bending roses
and the dripping grass.

Youth and Beauty

I bought a dishmop—
having no daughter—
for they had twisted
fine ribbons of shining copper
about white twine
and made a tousled head
of it, fastened it
upon a turned ash stick
slender at the neck
straight, tall—
when tied upright
on the brass wallbracket
to be a light for me
and naked
as a girl should seem
to her father.

The Thinker

My wife's new pink slippers
have gay pom-poms.
There is not a spot or a stain
on their satin toes or their sides.
All night they lie together
under her bed's edge.
Shivering I catch sight of them
and smile, in the morning.
Later I watch them
descending the stair,
hurrying through the doors
and round the table,
moving stiffly
with a shake of their gay pom-poms!
And I talk to them
in my secret mind
out of pure happiness.

The Tulip Bed

The May sun—whom
all things imitate—
that glues small leaves to
the wooden trees
shone from the sky
through bluegauze clouds
upon the ground.
Under the leafy trees
where the suburban streets
lay crossed,
with houses on each corner,
tangled shadows had begun
to join
the roadway and the lawns.
With excellent precision
the tulip bed
inside the iron fence
upreared its gaudy
yellow, white and red,
rimmed round with grass,
reposedly.

Spouts

In this world of
as fine a pair of breasts
as ever I saw
the fountain in
Madison Square
spouts up of water
a white tree
that dies and lives
as the rocking water
in the basin
turns from the stonerim
back upon the jet
and rising there
reflectively drops down again.

The Widow's Lament in Springtime

Sorrow is my own yard
where the new grass
flames as it has flamed
often before but not
with the cold fire
that closes round me this year.
Thirtyfive years
I lived with my husband.
The plumtree is white today
with masses of flowers.
Masses of flowers
load the cherry branches
and color some bushes
yellow and some red
but the grief in my heart
is stronger than they
for though they were my joy
formerly, today I notice them
and turned away forgetting.
Today my son told me
that in the meadows,
at the edge of the heavy woods
in the distance, he saw
trees of white flowers.
I feel that I would like
to go there
and fall into those flowers
and sink into the marsh near them.

The Nightingales

My shoes as I lean
unlacing them
stand out upon
flat worsted flowers.

Nimbly the shadows
of my fingers play
unlacing
over shoes and flowers.

Blueflags

I stopped the car
to let the children down
where the streets end
in the sun
at the marsh edge
and the reeds begin
and there are small houses
facing the reeds
and the blue mist
in the distance
with grapevine trellises
with grape clusters
small as strawberries
on the vines
and ditches
running springwater
that continue the gutters
with willows over them.
The reeds begin
like water at a shore
their pointed petals waving
dark green and light.
But blueflags are blossoming
in the reeds
which the children pluck
chattering in the reeds
high over their heads
which they part
with bare arms to appear
with fists of flowers
till in the air
there comes the smell
of calamus
from wet, gummy stalks.

Lighthearted William

Lighthearted William twirled
his November moustaches
and, half dressed, looked
from the bedroom window
upon the spring weather.

Heigh-ya! sighed he gaily
leaning out to see
up and down the street
where a heavy sunlight
lay beyond some blue shadows.

Into the room he drew
his head again and laughed
to himself quietly
twirling his green moustaches.

The Lonely Street

School is over. It is too hot
to walk at ease. At ease
in light frocks they walk the streets
to while the time away.
They have grown tall. They hold
pink flames in their right hands.
In white from head to foot,
with sidelong, idle look—
in yellow, floating stuff,
black sash and stockings—
touching their avid mouths
with pink sugar on a stick—
like a carnation each holds in her hand—
they mount the lonely street.

Portrait of the Author

The birches are mad with green points
the wood's edge is burning with their green,
burning, seething—No, no, no.
The birches are opening their leaves one
by one. Their delicate leaves unfold cold
and separate, one by one. Slender tassels
hang swaying from the delicate branch tips—
Oh, I cannot say it. There is no word.
Black is split at once into flowers. In
every bog and ditch, flares of
small fire, white flowers!—Agh,
the birches are mad, mad with their green.
The world is gone, torn into shreds
with this blessing. What have I left undone
that I should have undertaken?

O my brother, you redfaced, living man
ignorant, stupid whose feet are upon
this same dirt that I touch—and eat.
We are alone in this terror, alone,
face to face on this road, you and I,
wrapped by this flame!
Let the polished plows stay idle,
their gloss already on the black soil
But that face of yours—!
Answer me. I will clutch you. I
will hug you, grip you. I will poke my face
into your face and force you to see me.
Take me in your arms, tell me the commonest
thing that is in your mind to say,
say anything. I will understand you—!
It is the madness of the birch leaves opening
cold, one by one.

My rooms will receive me. But my rooms
are no longer sweet spaces where comfort
is ready to wait on me with its crumbs.
A darkness has brushed them. The mass
of yellow tulips in the bowl is shrunken.
Every familiar object is changed and dwarfed.
I am shaken, broken against a might
that splits comfort, blows apart
my careful partitions, crushes my house
and leaves me—with shrinking heart
and startled, empty eyes—peering out
into a cold world.

In the spring I would drink! In the spring
I would be drunk and lie forgetting all things.
Your face! Give me your face, Yang Kue Fei!
your hands, your lips to drink!
Give me your wrists to drink—
I drag you, I am drowned in you, you
overwhelm me! Drink!
Save me! The shad bush is in the edge
of the clearing. The yards in a fury
of lilac blossoms are driving me mad with terror.
Drink and lie forgetting the world.

And coldly the birch leaves are opening one by one.
Coldly I observe them and wait for the end.
And it ends.

The Great Figure

Among the rain
and lights
I saw the figure 5
in gold
on a red
firetruck
moving
tense
unheeded
to gong clangs
siren howls
and wheels rumbling
through the dark city.

Paterson

•

The Flower

Paterson

Before the grass is out the people are out
and bare twigs still whip the wind—
when there is nothing, in the pause between
snow and grass in the parks and at the street ends
—Say it, no ideas but in things—
nothing but the blank faces of the houses
and cylindrical trees
bent, forked by preconception and accident
split, furrowed, creased, mottled, stained
secret—into the body of the light—
These are the ideas, savage and tender
somewhat of the music, et cetera
of Paterson, that great philosopher—

From above, higher than the spires, higher
even than the office towers, from oozy fields
abandoned to grey beds of dead grass
black sumac, withered weed stalks
mud and thickets cluttered with dead leaves—
the river comes pouring in above the city
and crashes from the edge of the gorge
in a recoil of spray and rainbow mists—
—Say it, no ideas but in things—
and factories crystallized from its force,
like ice from spray upon the chimney rocks

. . . . . .

Say it! No ideas but in things. Mr.
Paterson has gone away
to rest and write. Inside the bus one sees
his thoughts sitting and standing. His thoughts
alight and scatter—

Who are these people (how complex
this mathematic) among whom I see myself
in the regularly ordered plateglass of
his thoughts, glimmering before shoes and bicycles—?
They walk incommunicado, the
equation is beyond solution, yet
its sense is clear—that they may live
his thought is listed in the Telephone
Directory—

        and there's young Alex Shorn
whose dad the boot-black bought a house
and painted it inside
with seascapes of a pale green monochrome—
the infant Dionysus springing from
Apollo's arm—the floors oakgrained in
Balkan fashion—Hermes' nose, the body
of a gourmand, the lips of Cupid, the eyes
the black eyes of Venus' sister—

But who! who are these people? It is
his flesh making the traffic, cranking the car
buying the meat—
Defeated in achieving the solution they
fall back among cheap pictures, furniture
filled silk, cardboard shoes, bad dentistry
windows that will not open, poisonous gin
scurvy, toothache—

        · · · · · ·

But never, in despair and anxiety
forget to drive wit in, in till it
discover that his thoughts are decorous and simple
and never forget that though his thoughts are decorous
and simple, the despair and anxiety

the grace and detail of
a dynamo—

Divine thought! Jacob fell backwards off the press
and broke his spine. What pathos, what mercy
of nurses (who keep birthday books)
and doctors who can't speak proper english—
is here correctly on a spotless bed
painless to the Nth power—the two legs
perfect without movement or sensation

Twice a month Paterson receives letters
from the Pope, his works are translated
into French, the clerks in the post office
ungum the rare stamps from his packages
and steal them for their children's albums

So in his high decorum he is wise

. . . . . .

What wind and sun of children stamping the snow
stamping the snow and screaming drunkenly
The actual, florid detail of cheap carpet
amazingly upon the floor and paid for
as no portrait ever was—Canary singing
and geraniums in tin cans spreading their leaves
reflecting red upon the frost—
They are the divisions and imbalances
of his whole concept, made small by pity
and desire, they are—no ideas beside the facts—

The Flower

A petal, colorless and without form
the oblong towers lie

beyond the low hill and northward the great
bridge stanchions,

small in the distance, have appeared,
pinkish and incomplete—

It is the city,
approaching over the river. Nothing

of it is mine, but visibly
for all that it is petal of a flower—my own.

It is a flower through which the wind
combs the whitened grass and a black dog

with yellow legs stands eating from a
garbage barrel. One petal goes eight blocks

past two churches and a brick school beyond
the edge of the park where under trees

leafless now, women having nothing else to do
sit in summer—to the small house

in which I happen to have been born. Or
a heap of dirt, if you care

to say it, frozen and sunstreaked in
the January sun, returning.

Then they hand you—they who wish to God
you'd keep your fingers out of

their business—science or philosophy or
anything else they can find to throw off

to distract you. But Madame Lenine
is a benefactress when under her picture

in the papers she is quoted as saying:
Children should be especially protected

from religion. Another petal
reaches to San Diego, California where

a number of young men, New Yorkers most
of them, are kicking up the dust.

A flower, at its heart (the stamens, pistil,
etc.) is a naked woman, about 38, just

out of bed, worth looking at both for
her body and her mind and what she has seen

and done. She it was put me straight
about the city when I said, It

makes me ill to see them run up
a new bridge like that in a few months

and I can't find time even to get
a book written. They have the power,

that's all, she replied. That's what you all
want. If you can't get it, acknowledge

at least what it is. And they're not
going to give it to you. Quite right.

For years I've been tormented by
that miracle, the buildings all lit up—

unable to say anything much to the point
though it is the major sight

of this region. But foolish to rhapsodize over
strings of lights, the blaze of a power

in which I have not the least part.
Another petal reaches

into the past, to Puerto Rico
when my mother was a child bathing in a small

river and splashing water up on
the yucca leaves to see them roll back pearls.

The snow is hard on the pavements. This
is no more a romance than an allegory.

I plan one thing—that I could press
buttons to do the curing of or caring for

the sick that I do laboriously now by hand
for cash, to have the time

when I am fresh, in the morning, when
my mind is clear and burning—to write.

Spring and All

Spring and All

By the road to the contagious hospital
under the surge of the blue
mottled clouds driven from the
northeast—a cold wind. Beyond, the
waste of broad, muddy fields
brown with dried weeds, standing and fallen

patches of standing water
the scattering of tall trees

All along the road the reddish
purplish, forked, upstanding, twiggy
stuff of bushes and small trees
with dead, brown leaves under them
leafless vines—

Lifeless in appearance, sluggish
dazed spring approaches—

They enter the new world naked,
cold, uncertain of all
save that they enter. All about them
the cold, familiar wind—

Now the grass, tomorrow
the stiff curl of wildcarrot leaf
One by one objects are defined—
It quickens: clarity, outline of leaf

But now the stark dignity of
entrance—Still, the profound change
has come upon them: rooted, they
grip down and begin to awaken

II

The Pot of Flowers

Pink confused with white
flowers and flowers reversed
take and spill the shaded flame
darting it back
into the lamp's horn

petals aslant darkened with mauve

red where in whorls
petal lays its glow upon petal
round flamegreen throats

petals radiant with transpiercing light
contending
                    above
the leaves
reaching up their modest green
from the pot's rim

and there, wholly dark, the pot
gay with rough moss.

III

The Farmer

The farmer in deep thought
is pacing through the rain
among his blank fields, with
hands in pockets,
in his head
the harvest already planted.
A cold wind ruffles the water
among the browned weeds.
On all sides
the world rolls coldly away:
black orchards
darkened by the March clouds—
leaving room for thought.
Down past the brushwood
bristling by
the rainsluiced wagonroad
looms the artist figure of
the farmer—composing
—antagonist

IV

Flight to the City

The Easter stars are shining
above lights that are flashing—
coronal of the black—
                              Nobody
to say it—
                Nobody to say: pinholes

Thither I would carry her

among the lights—

Burst it asunder
break through to the fifty words
necessary—

                a crown for her head with
castles upon it, skyscrapers
filled with nut-chocolates—

                              dovetame winds—
stars of tinsel

from the great end of a cornucopia
of glass.

V

The Black Winds

Black winds from the north
enter black hearts. Barred from
seclusion in lilies they strike
to destroy—

Beastly humanity
where the wind breaks it—

                          strident voices, heat
quickened, built of waves

Drunk with goats or pavements

Hate is of the night and the day
of flowers and rocks. Nothing
is gained by saying the night breeds
murder—It is the classical mistake

The day

All that enters in another person
all grass, all blackbirds flying
all azalea trees in flower
salt winds—

Sold to them men knock blindly together
splitting their heads open

That is why boxing matches and
Chinese poems are the same—That is why
Hartley praises Miss Wirt

There is nothing in the twist
of the wind but—dashes of cold rain

It is one with submarine vistas
purple and black fish turning
among undulant seaweed—

Black wind, I have poured my heart out
to you until I am sick of it—

Now I run my hand over you feeling
the play of your body—the quiver
of its strength—

The grief of the bowmen of Shu
moves nearer—There is
an approach with difficulty from
the dead—the winter casing of grief

How easy to slip
into the old mode, how hard to
cling firmly to the advance—

VI

To Have Done Nothing

No that is not it
nothing that I have done
nothing
I have done

is made up of
nothing
and the diphthong

ae

together with
the first person
singular
indicative

of the auxiliary
verb
to have

everything
I have done
is the same

if to do
is capable
of an
infinity of
combinations

involving the
moral
physical
and religious

codes

for everything
and nothing
are synonymous
when

energy *in vacuo*
has the power
of confusion

which only to
have done nothing
can make
perfect

VII

The Rose

The rose is obsolete
but each petal ends in
an edge, the double facet
cementing the grooved
columns of air—The edge
cuts without cutting
meets—nothing—renews
itself in metal or porcelain—

whither? It ends—

But if it ends
the start is begun
so that to engage roses
becomes a geometry—

Sharper, neater, more cutting
figured in majolica—
the broken plate
glazed with a rose

Somewhere the sense
makes copper roses
steel roses—

The rose carried weight of love
but love is at an end—of roses
It is at the edge of the
petal that love waits

Crisp, worked to defeat
laboredness—fragile
plucked, moist, half-raised
cold, precise, touching

What

The place between the petal's
edge and the

From the petal's edge a line starts
that being of steel
infinitely fine, infinitely
rigid penetrates
the Milky Way
without contact—lifting
from it—neither hanging
nor pushing—

The fragility of the flower
unbruised
penetrates space.

VIII

At the Faucet of June

The sunlight in a
yellow plaque upon the
varnished floor

is full of a song
inflated to
fifty pounds pressure

at the faucet of
June that rings
the triangle of the air

pulling at the
anemones in
Persephone's cow pasture—

When from among
the steel rocks leaps
J.P.M.

who enjoyed
extraordinary privileges
among virginity

to solve the core
of whirling flywheels
by cutting

the Gordian knot
with a Veronese or
perhaps a Rubens—

whose cars are about
the finest on
the market today—

And so it comes
to motor cars—
which is the son

leaving off the g
of sunlight and grass—
Impossible

to say, impossible
to underestimate—
wind, earthquakes in

Manchuria, a
partridge
from dry leaves.

Young Love

What about all this writing?

O "Kiki"
O Miss Margaret Jarvis
The backhandspring
I: clean
   clean
   clean: yes . . New York

Wrigley's, appendicitis, John Marin:
skyscraper soup—

Either that or a bullet!

Once
anything might have happened
You lay relaxed on my knees—
the starry night
spread out warm and blind
above the hospital—

Pah!

It is unclean
which is not straight to the mark—

In my life the furniture eats me

the chairs, the floor
the walls
which heard your sobs

drank up my emotion—
they which alone know everything

and snitched on us in the morning—

What to want?

Drunk we go forward surely
Not I

beds, beds, beds
elevators, fruit, night-tables
breasts to see, white and blue—
to hold in the hand, to nozzle

It is not onion soup
Your sobs soaked through the walls
breaking the hospital to pieces
Everything
—windows, chairs
obscenely drunk, spinning—
white, blue, orange
—hot with our passion
wild tears, desperate rejoinders
my legs, turning slowly
end over end in the air!

But what would you have?

All I said was:
there, you see, it is broken
stockings, shoes, hairpins
your bed, I wrapped myself round you—

I watched.

You sobbed, you beat your pillow
you tore your hair
you dug your nails into your sides

I was your nightgown
                   I watched!

Clean is he alone
after whom stream
the broken pieces of the city—
flying apart at his approaches

but I merely
caressed you curiously
fifteen years ago and you still
go about the city, they say
patching up sick school children

X

The Eyeglasses

The universality of things
draws me toward the candy
with melon flowers that open

about the edge of refuse
proclaiming without accent
the quality of the farmer's

shoulders and his daughter's
accidental skin, so sweet
with clover and the small

yellow cinquefoil in the
parched places. It is
this that engages the favorable

distortion of eyeglasses
that see everything and remain
related to mathematics—

in the most practical frame of
brown celluloid made to
represent tortoiseshell—

A letter from the man who
wants to start a new magazine
made of linen

and he owns a typewriter—
July 1, 1922
All this is for eyeglasses

to discover. But
they lie there with the gold
earpieces folded down

tranquilly Titicaca—

The Right of Way

In passing with my mind
on nothing in the world

but the right of way
I enjoy on the road by

virtue of the law—
I saw

an elderly man who
smiled and looked away

to the north past a house—
a woman in blue

who was laughing and
leaning forward to look up

into the man's half
averted face

and a boy of eight who was
looking at the middle of

the man's belly
at a watchchain—

The supreme importance
of this nameless spectacle

sped me by them
without a word—

Why bother where I went?
for I went spinning on the

four wheels of my car
along the wet road until

I saw a girl with one leg
over the rail of a balcony

Composition

The red paper box
hinged with cloth

is lined
inside and out
with imitation
leather

It is the sun
the table
with dinner
on it for
these are the same

Its twoinch trays
have engineers
that convey glue
to airplanes

or for old ladies
that darn socks
paper clips
and red elastics—

What is the end
to insects
that suck gummed
labels?

for this is eternity
through its

dial we discover
transparent tissue
on a spool

But the stars
are round
cardboard
with a tin edge

and a ring
to fasten them
to a trunk
for the vacation—

XIII

The Agonized Spires

Crustaceous
wedge
of sweaty kitchens
on rock
overtopping
thrusts of the sea

Waves of steel
from swarming backstreets
shell
of coral
inventing
electricity—

Lights
speckle
El Greco
lakes
in renaissance
twilight
with triphammers

which pulverize
nitrogen
of old pastures
to dodge
motorcars
with arms and legs—

The aggregate
is untamed

encapsulating
irritants
but
of agonized spires
knits
peace

where bridge stanchions
rest
certainly
piercing
left ventricles
with long
sunburnt fingers

XIV

Death the Barber

Of death
the barber
the barber
talked to me

cutting my
life with
sleep to trim
my hair—

It's just
a moment
he said, we die
every night—

And of
the newest
ways to grow
hair on

bald death—
I told him
of the quartz
lamp

and of old men
with third
sets of teeth
to the cue

of an old man
who said
at the door—
Sunshine today!

for which
death shaves
him twice
a week

Light Becomes Darkness

The decay of cathedrals
is efflorescent
through the phenomenal
growth of movie houses

whose catholicity is
progress since
destruction and creation
are simultaneous

without sacrifice
of even the smallest
detail even to the
volcanic organ whose

woe is translatable
to joy if light becomes
darkness and darkness
light, as it will—

But schism which seems
adamant is diverted
from the perpendicular
by simply rotating the object

cleaving away the root of
disaster which it
seemed to foster. Thus
the movies are a moral force

Nightly the crowds
with the closeness and

universality of sand
witness the selfpittle

which used to be drowned
in incense and intoned
over by the supple-jointed
imagination of inoffensiveness

backed by biblical
rigidity made into passion plays
upon the altar to
attract the dynamic mob

whose female relative
sweeping grass Tolstoi
saw injected into
the Russian nobility.

To an Old Jaundiced Woman

O tongue
licking
the sore on
her netherlip

O toppled belly

O passionate cotton
stuck with
matted hair

elsian slobber
upon
the folded handkerchief

I can't die

—moaned the old
jaundiced woman
rolling her
saffron eyeballs

I can't die
I can't die

XVII

Shoot it Jimmy!

Our orchestra
is the cat's nuts—

Banjo jazz
with a nickelplated

amplifier to
soothe

the savage beast—
Get the rhythm

That sheet stuff
's a lot a cheese.

Man
gimme the key

and lemme loose—
I make 'em crazy

with my harmonies—
Shoot it Jimmy

Nobody
Nobody else

but me—
They can't copy it

269

XVIII

To Elsie

The pure products of America
go crazy—
mountain folk from Kentucky

or the ribbed north end of
Jersey
with its isolate lakes and

valleys, its deaf-mutes, thieves
old names
and promiscuity between

devil-may-care men who have taken
to railroading
out of sheer lust of adventure—

and young slatterns, bathed
in filth
from Monday to Saturday

to be tricked out that night
with gauds
from imaginations which have no

peasant traditions to give them
character
but flutter and flaunt

sheer rags—succumbing without
emotion
save numbed terror

under some hedge of choke-cherry
or viburnum—
which they cannot express—

Unless it be that marriage
perhaps
with a dash of Indian blood

will throw up a girl so desolate
so hemmed round
with disease or murder

that she'll be rescued by an
agent—
reared by the state and

sent out at fifteen to work in
some hard-pressed
house in the suburbs—

some doctor's family, some Elsie—
voluptuous water
expressing with broken

brain the truth about us—
her great
ungainly hips and flopping breasts

addressed to cheap
jewelry
and rich young men with fine eyes

as if the earth under our feet
were
an excrement of some sky

and we degraded prisoners
destined
to hunger until we eat filth

while the imagination strains
after deer
going by fields of goldenrod in

the stifling heat of September
Somehow
it seems to destroy us

It is only in isolate flecks that
something
is given off

No one
to witness
and adjust, no one to drive the car

XIX

Horned Purple

This is the time of year
when boys fifteen and seventeen
wear two horned lilac blossoms
in their caps—or over one ear

What is it that does this?

It is a certain sort—
drivers for grocers or taxidrivers
white and colored—

fellows that let their hair grow long
in a curve over one eye—

Horned purple

Dirty satyrs, it is
vulgarity raised to the last power

They have stolen them
broken the bushes apart
with a curse for the owner—

Lilacs—

They stand in the doorways
on the business streets with a sneer
on their faces

adorned with blossoms

Out of their sweet heads
dark kisses—rough faces

The Sea

The sea that encloses her young body
ula lu la lu
is the sea of many arms—

The blazing secrecy of noon is undone
and and and
the broken sand is the sound of love—

The flesh is firm that turns in the sea
O la la
the sea that is cold with dead men's tears—

Deeply the wooing that penetrated
to the edge of the sea
returns in the plash of the waves—

a wink over the shoulder
large as the ocean—
with wave following wave to the edge

coom barroom—

It is the cold of the sea
broken upon the sand by the force
of the moon—

In the sea the young flesh playing
floats with the cries of far off men
who rise in the sea

with green arms
to homage again the fields over there
where the night is deep—

la lu la lu
but lips too few
assume the new—marruu

Underneath the sea where it is dark
there is no edge
so two—

XXI

The Red Wheelbarrow

so much depends
upon

a red wheel
barrow

glazed with rain
water

beside the white
chickens.

XXII

Quietness

one day in Paradise
a Gypsy

smiled
to see the blandness

of the leaves—
so many

so lascivious
and still

XXIII

Rigamarole

The veritable night
of wires and stars

the moon is in
the oak tree's crotch

and sleepers in
the windows cough

athwart the round
and pointed leaves

and insects sting
while on the grass

the whitish moonlight
tearfully

assumes the attitudes
of afternoon—

But it is real
where peaches hang

recalling death's
long-promised symphony

whose tuneful wood
and stringish undergrowth

are ghosts existing
without being

save to come with juice
and pulp to assuage

the hungers which
the night reveals

so that now at last
the truth's aglow

with devilish peace
forestalling day

which dawns tomorrow
with dreadful reds

the heart to predicate
with mists that loved

the ocean and the fields—
Thus moonlight

is the perfect
human touch.

The Avenue of Poplars

The leaves embrace
in the trees

it is a wordless
world

without personality
I do not

seek a path
I am still with

Gypsy lips pressed
to my own—

It is the kiss
of leaves

without being
poison ivy

or nettle, the kiss
of oak leaves—

He who has kissed
a leaf

need look no further—
I ascend

through
a canopy of leaves

and at the same time
I descend

for I do nothing
unusual—

I ride in my car
I think about

prehistoric caves
in the Pyrenees—

the cave of
Les Trois Frères

Rapid Transit

Somebody dies every four minutes
in New York State—

To hell with you and your poetry—
You will rot and be blown
through the next solar system
with the rest of the gases—

What the hell do you know about it?

AXIOMS

Don't get killed

Careful Crossing Campaign
Cross Crossings Cautiously

THE HORSES   black
                          &
PRANCED   white

Outings in New York City

Ho for the open country

Don't stay shut up in hot rooms
Go to one of the Great Parks
Pelham Bay for example

It's on Long Island Sound
with bathing, boating
tennis, baseball, golf, etc.

Acres and acres of green grass
wonderful shade trees, rippling brooks

    Take the Pelham Bay Park Branch
    of the Lexington Ave. (East Side)
    Line and you are there in a few
    minutes

Interborough Rapid Transit Co.

XXVI

At the Ball Game

The crowd at the ball game
is moved uniformly

by a spirit of uselessness
which delights them—

all the exciting detail
of the chase

and the escape, the error
the flash of genius—

all to no end save beauty
the eternal—

So in detail they, the crowd,
are beautiful

for this
to be warned against

saluted and defied—
It is alive, venomous

it smiles grimly
its words cut—

The flashy female with her
mother, gets it—

284

The Jew gets it straight—it
is deadly, terrifying—

It is the Inquisition, the
Revolution

It is beauty itself
that lives

day by day in them
idly—

This is
the power of their faces

It is summer, it is the solstice
the crowd is

cheering, the crowd is laughing
in detail

permanently, seriously
without thought

The Hermaphroditic Telephones

Warm rains
wash away winter's
hermaphroditic telephones

whose demonic bells
piercing the torpid
ground

have filled with circular
purple and green
and blue anemonies

the radiant nothing
of crystalline
spring.

XXVIII

The Wildflower

Black eyed susan
rich orange
round the purple core

the white daisy
is not enough

Crowds are white
as farmers
who live poorly

But you
are rich
in savagery—

Arab
Indian
dark woman.

Struggle of Wings

Struggle of Wings

Roundclouds occluding patches of the
sky rival steam bluntly towering,
slowspinning billows which rival
the resting snow, which rivals the sun

beaten out upon it, flashing
to a struggle (of wings) which
fills the still air—still
but cold—yet burning . . .

It is the snow risen upon itself, it is
winter pressed breast to breast
with its own whiteness, transparent
yet visible:

Together, with their pigeon's heads whose
stupid eyes deceive no one—
they hold up between them something
which wants to fall to the ground . . .

And there's the river with thin ice upon it
fanning out half over the black
water, the free middlewater racing under its
ripples that move crosswise on the stream

But the wings and bodies of the pigeonlike
creatures keep fluttering, turning together
hiding that which is between them. It seems
to rest not in their claws but upon their breasts—

It is a baby!
Now it is very clear (*) they're keeping the child
(naked in the air) warm and safe between them.
The eyes of the birds are fixed in

a bestial ecstasy. They strive together panting.
It is an antithesis of logic, very
theoretical. To his face the baby claps
the bearded face of Socrates . . .

Ho, ho! he's dropped it. It was a mask.
Now indeed the encounter throws aside all dissim-
ulation. The false birdheads drop back, arms
spring from the wingedges, all the parts

of two women become distinct, the anatomy
familiar and complete to the smallest detail:
A meaning plainly antipoetical . . . and
. . . all there is is won

(. . . . .

It is Poesy, born of a man and two women
Exit No. 4, the string from the windowshade
has a noose at the bottom, a noose? or
a ring—bound with a white cord, knotted
around the circumference in a design—
                              And all there is is won

And it is Innes on the meadows and fruit is
yellow ripening in windows every minute
growing brighter in the bulblight by the
cabbages and spuds—
                              And all there is is won

What are black 4 a.m.'s after all but black
4 a.m.'s like anything else: a tree
a fork, a leaf, a pane of glass—?
                              And all there is is won

A relic of old decency, a "very personal friend"
                              And all there is is won

(Envoi)

Pic, your crows feed at your window sill
asso, try and get near mine . . .
                            And all there is is won
                            (. . . . .

                                                    All

up and down the Rio Grand the sand is sand
on every hand (Grand chorus and finale)
                            (. . . . .

Out of such drab trash as this
by a metamorphosis
bright as wallpaper or crayon
or where the sun casts ray on ray on
flowers in a dish, you shall weave
for Poesy a gaudy sleeve
a scarf, a cap and find him gloves
whiter than the backs of doves

                    . . . .

                                        Clothe him

richly, those who loathe him
will besmirch him fast enough.
A surcease to sombre stuff—
black's black, black's one thing
but he's not a blackbird. Bring
something else for him to wear.
See! he's young he has black hair!
Very well then, a red vest . . .

The Descent of Winter

The Descent of Winter

9/29

My bed is narrow
in a small room
at sea

The numbers are on
the wall
Arabic I

Berth No. 2
was empty above me
the steward

took it apart
and removed
it

only the number
remains
· 2 ·

on an oval disc
of celluloid
tacked

to the white-enameled
woodwork
with

two bright nails
like stars
beside

297

the moon

9/30

There are no perfect waves—
Your writings are a sea
full of misspellings and
faulty sentences. Level. Troubled

A center distant from the land
touched by the wings
of nearly silent birds
that never seem to rest—

This is the sadness of the sea—
waves like words, all broken—
a sameness of lifting and falling mood.

I lean watching the detail
of brittle crest, the delicate
imperfect foam, yellow weed
one piece like another—

There is no hope—if not a coral
island slowly forming
to wait for birds to drop
the seeds will make it habitable

10/9

and there's a little blackboy
in a doorway
scratching his wrists

The cap on his head
is red and blue
with a broad peak to it

and his mouth
is open, his tongue
between his teeth—

10/10

Monday
            the canna flaunts
its crimson head

crimson lying folded
crisply down upon

                        the invisible

darkly crimson heart
of this poor yard

the grass is long

                        October tenth
1927

10/21

In the dead weeds a rubbish heap
aflame: the orange flames
stream horizontal, windblown
they parallel the ground

waving up and down
the flamepoints alternating
the body streaked with loops
and purple stains while
the pale smoke, above
steadily continues eastward—

What chance have the old?
There are no duties for them
no places where they may sit
their knowledge is laughed at
they cannot see, they cannot hear.
A small bundle on the shoulders
weighs them down
one hand is put back under it
to hold it steady.
Their feet hurt, they are weak
they should not have to suffer
as younger people must and do
there should be a truce for them

                    10/22

        that brilliant field
        of rainwet orange
        blanketed

        by the red grass
        and oilgreen bayberry

        the last yarrow
        on the gutter
        white by the sandy
        rainwater

and a white birch
with yellow leaves
and few
and loosely hung

and a young dog
jumped out
of the old barrel

10/28

On hot days
the sewing machine
                whirling

        in the next room
        in the kitchen

and men at the bar
        talking of the strike
        and cash

10/28

in this strong light
the leafless beechtree
shines like a cloud

it seems to glow
of itself
with a soft stript light
of love
over the brittle
grass

But there are
on second look
a few yellow leaves
still shaking

far apart

just one here one there
trembling vividly

10/29

The justice of poverty
    its shame its dirt
are one with the meanness
    of love

its organ its tarpaulin
    the green birds
the fat sleepy horse
    the old men

the grinder sourfaced
    hat over eyes
the beggar smiling all open
    the lantern out

and the popular tunes—
    sold to the least bidder
for a nickel
    two cents or

nothing at all or even
    against the desire
forced on us

To freight cars in the air

all the slow
    clank, clank
    clank, clank
moving above the treetops

the
    wha, wha
of the hoarse whistle

    pah,   pah,   pah
    pah, pah, pah, pah, pah
    piece and piece
    piece and piece
moving still trippingly
through the morningmist

long after the engine
has fought by
          and disappeared
in silence
          to the left

11/1

The moon, the dried weeds
and the Pleiades—

Seven feet tall
the dark, dried weedstalks
make a part of the night
a red lace
on the blue milky sky

303

Write—
by a small lamp

the Pleiades are almost
nameless
and the moon is tilted
and halfgone

And in runningpants and
with ecstatic, aesthetic faces
on the illumined
signboard are leaping
over printed hurdles and
"¼ of their energy comes from bread"

two
gigantic highschool boys
ten feet tall

11/2

Dahlias—
    What a red
        and yellow and white
mirror to the sun, round
        and petaled
        is this she holds?
        with a red face
all in black
        and grey hair
        sticking out
    from under the bonnet brim
Is this Washington Avenue Mr. please
        or do I have to
        cross the tracks?

A MORNING IMAGINATION OF RUSSIA

The earth and the sky were very close
When the sun rose it rose in his heart
It bathed the red cold world of
the dawn so that the chill was his own
The mists were sleep and sleep began
to fade from his eyes, below him in the
garden a few flowers were lying forward
on the intense green grass where
in the opalescent shadows oak leaves
were pressed hard down upon it in patches
by the night rain. There were no cities
between him and his desires
his hatreds and his loves were without walls
without rooms, without elevators
without files, delays of veiled murderers
muffled thieves, the tailings of
tedious, dead pavements, the walls
against desire save only for him who can pay
high, there were no cities—he was
without money—

                 Cities had faded richly
into foreign countries, stolen from Russia—
the richness of her cities—

Scattered wealth was close to his heart
he felt it uncertainly beating at
that moment in his wrists, scattered
wealth—but there was not much at hand

Cities are full of light, fine clothes
delicacies for the table, variety,
novelty—fashion: all spent for this.

Never to be like that again:
the frame that was. It tickled his
imagination. But it passed in a rising calm

Tan dar a dei; Tan dar a dei!

He was singing. Two miserable peasants
very lazy and foolish
seemed to have walked out from his own
feet and were walking away with wooden rakes
under the six nearly bare poplars, up the hill

There go my feet.

He stood still in the window forgetting
to shave—

The very old past was refound
redirected. It had wandered into himself
The world was himself, these were
his own eyes that were seeing, his own mind
that was straining to comprehend, his own
hands that would be touching other hands
They were his own!
His own, feeble, uncertain. He would go
out to pick herbs, he graduate of
the old university. He would go out
and ask that old woman, in the little
village by the lake, to show him wild
ginger. He himself would not know the plant.

A horse was stepping up the dirt road
under his window

He decided not to shave. Like those two
that he knew now, as he had never

known them formerly. A city, fashion
had been between—

Nothing between now.

He would go to the soviet unshaven. This
was the day—and listen. Listen. That
was all he did, listen to them, weigh
for them. He was turning into
a pair of scales, the scales in the
zodiac.

   But closer, he was himself
the scales. The local soviet. They could
weigh. If it was not too late. He felt
uncertain many days. But all were uncertain
together and he must weigh for them out
of himself.

   He took a small pair of scissors
from the shelf and clipped his nails
carefully. He himself served the fire.

We have cut out the cancer but
who knows? perhaps the patient will die
the patient is anybody, anything
worthless that I desire, my hands
to have it—instead of the feeling
that there is a piece of glazed paper
between me and the paper—invisible
but tough running through the legal
processes of possession—a city, that
we could possess—

   It's in art, it's in
the French school.

What we lacked was
everything. It is the middle of
everything. Not to have.

We have little now but
we have that. We are convalescents. Very
feeble. Our hands shake. We need a
transfusion. No one will give it to us,
they are afraid of infection. I do not
blame them. We have paid heavily. But we
have gotten—touch. The eyes and the ears
down on it. Close.

11/7

We must listen. Before
she died she told them—
I always liked to be well dressed
I wanted to look nice—

So she asked them to dress
her well. They curled her hair . . .

Now she fought
She didn't want to go
She didn't want to!

11/8

O river of my heart polluted
and defamed I have compared you
to that other lying in
the red November grass

beginning to be cleaned now
from factory pollution

Though at night a watchman
must still prowl lest some paid hand
open the waste sluices—

That river will be clean
before ever you will be

11/10

The shell flowers
the wax grapes and peaches
the fancy oak or mahogany tables
the highbacked baronial chairs

Or the girls' legs
agile stanchions
the breasts
the pinheads—

—Wore my bathing suit
wet
four hours after sundown.
That's how. Yea?
Easy to get
hard to get rid of.

Then unexpectedly
a small house with a soaring oak
leafless above it

Someone should summarize these things
in the interest of local

government or how
a spotted dog goes up a gutter—

and in chalk crudely
upon the railroad bridge support
a woman rampant
brandishing two rolling pins

11/20

Even idiots grow old
   in a cap with a peak
over his right ear
   cross-eyed
shamble-footed
   minding the three goats
behind the firehouse
   his face is deeper lined
than last year
   and the rain comes down
in gusts suddenly

11/22

and hunters still return
even through the city
with their guns slung
openly from the shoulder
emptyhanded howbeit
for the most part
         but aloof
as if from and truly from
another older world

I make really very little money.
What of it?
I prefer the grass with the rain on it
the short grass before my headlights
when I am turning the car—
a degenerate trait, no doubt.
It would ruin England.

What an image in the face of Almighty God is she
her hands in her slicker pockets, head bowed,
Tam pulled down, flat-backed, lanky-legged,
loose feet kicking the pebbles as she goes

Impromptu: The Suckers

Impromptu: The Suckers

Take it out in vile whisky, take it out
in lifting your skirts to show your silken
crotches; it is this that is intended.
You are it. Your pleas will always be denied.
You too will always go up with the two guys,
scapegoats to save the Republic and
especially the State of Massachusetts. The
Governor says so and you ain't supposed
to ask for details—

Your case has been reviewed by high-minded
and unprejudiced observers (like hell
they were!) the president of a great
university, the president of a noteworthy
technical school and a judge too old to sit
on the bench, men already rewarded for
their services to pedagogy and the enforcement
of arbitrary statutes. In other words
pimps to tradition—

Why in hell didn't they choose some other
kind of "unprejudiced adviser" for their
death council? instead of sticking to that
autocratic strain of Boston backwash, except
that the council was far from unprejudiced
but the product of a rejected, discredited
class long since outgrown except for use in
courts and school, and that they
wanted it so—

Why didn't they choose at least one decent
Jew or some fair-minded Negro or anybody
but such a triumvirate of inversion, the

New England aristocracy, bent on working off
a grudge against you, Americans, you
are the suckers, you are the ones who will
be going up on the eleventh to get the current
shot into you, for the glory of the state
and the perpetuation of abstract justice—

And all this in the face of the facts: that
the man who swore, and deceived the jury
wilfully by so doing, that the bullets found
in the bodies of the deceased could be
identified as having been fired from the pistol
of one of the accused—later
acknowledged that he could not so identify
them; that the jurors now seven years after
the crime do not remember the details and
have wanted to forget them; that the
prosecution has never succeeded in
apprehending the accomplices nor in connecting
the prisoners with any of the loot stolen—

The case is perfect against you, all the
documents say so—in spite of the fact that
it is reasonably certain that you were not
at the scene of the crime, shown, quite as
convincingly as the accusing facts in the
court evidence, by better reasoning to have
been committed by someone else with whom
the loot can be connected and among whom the
accomplices can be found—

It's no use, you are Americans, just the dregs.
It's all you deserve. You've got the cash,
what the hell do you care? You've got
nothing to lose. You are inheritors of a great
tradition. My country right or wrong!

You do what you're told to do. You don't
answer back the way Tommy Jeff did or Ben
Frank or Georgie Washing. I'll say you
don't. You're civilized. You let your
betters tell you where you get off. Go
ahead—

But after all, the thing that swung heaviest
against you was that you were scared when
they copped you. Explain that you
nature's nobleman! For you know that every
American is innocent and at peace in his
own heart. He hasn't a damned thing to be
afraid of. He knows the government is for
him. Why, when a cop steps up and grabs
you at night you just laugh and think it's
a hell of a good joke—

This is what was intended from the first.
So take it out in your rotten whisky and
silk underwear. That's what you get out of
it. But put it down in your memory that this
is the kind of stuff that they can't get away
with. It is there and it's loaded. No one
can understand what makes the present age
what it is. They are mystified by certain
insistences.

Collected Poems 1934

All the Fancy Things

         music and painting and all that
         That's all they thought of
         in Puerto Rico in the old Spanish
         days when she was a girl

         So that now
         she doesn't know what to do

         with herself alone
         and growing old up here—

         Green is green
         but the tag ends
         of older things, *ma chère*

         must withstand rebuffs
         from that which returns
         to the beginnings—

         Or what? a
         clean air, high up, unoffended
         by gross odors

Hemmed-in Males

The saloon is gone up the creek
with the black sand round its
mouth, it went floating like

a backhouse on the Mississippi in
flood time but it went up
the creek into Limbo from whence

only empty bottles ever return
and that's where George is
He's gone upstream to ask 'em

to let him in at the hole
in the wall where the W.C.T.U.
sits knitting elastic stockings

for varicose veins. Poor George
he's got a job now as janitor
in Lincoln School but the saloon

is gone forever with pictures
of Sullivan and Kilrain on
the walls and Pop Anson holding

a bat. Poor George, they've cut
out his pituitary gland and his
vas deferens is in the spittoon—

You can laugh at him without his
organs but that's the way with
a river when it wants to

drown you, it sucks you in and
you feel the old saloon sinking
under you and you say good-by

just as George did, good-by poetry
the black sand's got me, the old
days are over, there's no place

any more for me to go now
except home—

Brilliant Sad Sun

Lee's
Lunch

Spaghetti   Oysters
a Specialty   Clams

and raw Winter's done
to a turn—Restaurant: Spring!
Ah, Madam, what good are your thoughts

romantic but true
beside this gaiety of the sun
and that huge appetite?

Look!
from a glass pitcher she serves
clear water to the white chickens.

What are your memories
beside that purity?
The empty pitcher dangling

from her grip
her coarse voice croaks
Bon jor'

And Patti, on her first concert tour
sang at your house in Mayaguez
and your brother was there

What beauty
beside your sadness—and
what sorrow

It Is a Living Coral

a trouble

archaically fettered
to produce

E Pluribus Unum an
island

in the sea a Capitol
surmounted

by Armed Liberty—
painting

sculpture straddled by
a dome

eight million pounds
in weight

iron plates constructed
to expand

and contract with
variations

of temperature
the folding

and unfolding of a lily.
And Congress

authorized and the
Commission

was entrusted was
entrusted!

a sculptured group
Mars

in Roman mail placing
a wreath

of laurel on the brow
of Washington

Commerce Minerva
Thomas

Jefferson John Hancock
at

the table Mrs. Motte
presenting

Indian burning arrows
to Generals

Marion and Lee to fire
her mansion

and dislodge the British—
this scaleless

jumble is superb

and accurate in its
expression

of the thing they
would destroy—

Baptism of Poca-
hontas

with a little card
hanging

under it to tell
the persons

in the picture.

It climbs

it runs, it is Geo.
Shoup

of Idaho it wears
a beard

it fetches naked
Indian

women from a river
Trumbull

Varnum Henderson
Frances

Willard's corset is
absurd—

Banks White Columbus
stretched

in bed men felling trees

The Hon. Michael
C. Kerr

onetime Speaker of
the House

of Representatives
Perry

in a rowboat on Lake
Erie

changing ships the
dead

among the wreckage
sickly green

To

a child (a boy) bouncing
a ball (a blue ball)—

He bounces it (a toy racket
in his hand) and runs

and catches it (with his
left hand) six floors

straight down—
which is the old back yard

This Florida: 1924

of which I am the sand—
one of the sands—in which
the turtle eggs are baking—

The people are running away
toward me, Hibiscus,
where I lie, sad,

by the stern
slaying palm trees—
(They're so much better

at a distance than they are
up close. Cocoanuts
aren't they?

or Royal palms?
They are so tall the wind
rips them to shreds)

—this frightened
frantic pilgrimage has left
my bungalows up here

lonely as the Lido in April
"Florida the Flowery!"
Well,

it's a kind of borrowed
pleasure after all (as at the movies)
to see them

tearing off to escape it
this winter
this winter that I feel

So—
already ten o'clock?
Vorwärts!

e-e i-i o-o u-u a-a
Shall I write it in iambs?
Cottages in a row

all radioed and showerbathed?
But I am sick of rime—
The whole damned town

is riming up one street
and down another, yet there is
the rime of her white teeth

the rime of glasses
at my plate, the ripple time
the rime her fingers make—

And we thought to escape rime
by imitation of the senseless
unarrangement of wild things—

the stupidest rime of all—
Rather, Hibiscus,
let me examine

those varying shades
of orange, clear as an electric
bulb on fire

or powdery with sediment—
matt, the shades and textures
of a Cubist picture

the charm
of fish by Hartley, orange
of ale and lilies

orange of topaz, orange of red hair
orange of curaçoa
orange of the Tiber

turbid, orange of the bottom
rocks in Maine rivers
orange of mushrooms

of Cepes that Marshal loved
to cook in copper
pans, orange of the sun—

I shall do my pees, instead—
boiling them in test tubes
holding them to the light

dropping in the acid—
Peggy has a little albumen
in hers—

Young Sycamore

I must tell you
this young tree
whose round and firm trunk
between the wet

pavement and the gutter
(where water
is trickling) rises
bodily

into the air with
one undulant
thrust half its height—
and then

dividing and waning
sending out
young branches on
all sides—

hung with cocoons
it thins
till nothing is left of it
but two

eccentric knotted
twigs
bending forward
hornlike at the top

The Cod Head

Miscellaneous weed
strands, stems, debris—
firmament

to fishes—
where the yellow feet
of gulls dabble

oars whip
ships churn to bubbles—
at night wildly

agitate phospores-
cent midges—but by day
flaccid

moons in whose
discs sometimes a red cross
lives—four

fathom—the bottom skids
a mottle of green
sands backward—

amorphous waver-
ing rocks—three fathom
the vitreous

body through which—
small scudding fish deep
down—and

now a lulling lift
and fall—
red stars—a severed cod—

head between two
green stones—lifting
falling

New England

is a condition—
of bedrooms whose electricity

is brickish or made into
T beams—They dangle them

on wire cables to the tops
of Woolworth buildings

five and ten cents worth—
There they have bolted them

into place at masculine risk—
Or a boy with a rose under

the lintel of his cap
standing to have his picture

taken on the butt of a girder
with the city a mile down—

captured, lonely cock atop
iron girders wears rosepetal

smile—a thought of Indians
on chestnut branches

to end "walking on the air"

The Bull

It is in captivity—
ringed, haltered, chained
to a drag
the bull is godlike

Unlike the cows
he lives alone, nozzles
the sweet grass gingerly
to pass the time away

He kneels, lies down
and stretching out
a foreleg licks himself
about the hoof

then stays
with half-closed eyes,
Olympian commentary on
the bright passage of days.

—The round sun
smooth his lacquer
through
the glossy pinetrees

his substance hard
as ivory or glass—
through which the wind
yet plays—
                    milkless

he nods
the hair between his horns
and eyes matted
with hyacinthine curls

In the 'Sconset Bus

Upon the fallen
cheek

a gauzy down—
And on

the nape
—indecently

a mat
of yellow hair

stuck with
celluloid

pins
not quite

matching it
—that's

two shades
darker

at the roots
Hanging

from the ears
the hooks

piercing the
flesh—

gold and semi-
precious

stones—
And in her

lap the dog
(Youth)

resting
his head on

the ample
shoulder his

bright
mouth agape

pants restlessly
backward

Poem

As the cat
climbed over
the top of

the jamcloset
first the right
forefoot

carefully
then the hind
stepped down

into the pit of
the empty
flowerpot

Sluggishly

or with a rush
the river flows—

and none
is unaffected—

       Think:
the clear stream

boiling at
the boat's wake

or—
   a stench
your choice is—

And respond?

       crapulous
—having eaten

fouling
the water grass

The Jungle

It is not the still weight
of the trees, the
breathless interior of the wood,
tangled with wrist-thick

vines, the flies, reptiles,
the forever fearful monkeys
screaming and running
in the branches—

              but
a girl waiting
shy, brown, soft-eyed—
to guide you
            Upstairs, sir.

Between Walls

the back wings
of the

hospital where
nothing

will grow lie
cinders

in which shine
the broken

pieces of a green
bottle

The Lily

The branching head of
tiger-lilies through the window
in the air—

A humming bird
is still on whirring wings
above the flowers—

By spotted petals curling back
and tongues that hang
the air is seen—

It's raining—
water's caught
among the curled-back petals

Caught and held
and there's a fly—
are blossoming

On Gay Wallpaper

The green-blue ground
is ruled with silver lines
to say the sun is shining

And on this moral sea
of grass or dreams lie flowers
or baskets of desires

Heaven knows what they are
between cerulean shapes
laid regularly round

Mat roses and tridentate
leaves of gold
threes, threes and threes

Three roses and three stems
the basket floating
standing in the horns of blue

Repeated to the ceiling
to the windows
where the day

Blows in
the scalloped curtains to
the sound of rain

The Source

The slope of the heavy woods
pales and disappears
in the wall of mist that hides

the edge above whose peak
last night the moon—

But it is morning and a new light
marks other things
a pasture which begins

where silhouettes of scrub
and balsams stand uncertainly

On whose green three maples
are distinctly pressed
beside a red barn

with new shingles in the old
all cancelled by

A triple elm's inverted
lichen mottled
triple thighs from which

wisps of twigs
droop with sharp leaves

Which shake in the crotch
brushing the stained bark
fitfully

Beyond which lies
the profound detail of the woods
restless, distressed

soft underfoot
the low ferns

Mounting a rusty root
the pungent mould
globular fungi

water in an old
hoof print

Cow dung and in
the uneven aisles of
the trees

rock strewn a stone
half-green

A spring in whose depth
white sand bubbles
overflows

clear under late raspberries
and delicate-stemmed touch-me-nots

Where alders follow it marking
the low ground
the water is cast upon

a stair of uneven stones
with a rustling sound

An edge of bubbles stirs
swiftness is moulded
speed grows

the profuse body advances
over the stones unchanged

Nantucket

Flowers through the window
lavender and yellow

changed by white curtains—
Smell of cleanliness—

Sunshine of late afternoon—
On the glass tray

a glass pitcher, the tumbler
turned down, by which

a key is lying—And the
immaculate white bed

The Winds

flowing edge to edge
their clear edges meeting—
the winds of this northern March—
blow the bark from the trees
the soil from the field
the hair from the heads of
girls, the shirts from the backs
of the men, roofs from the
houses, the cross from the
church, clouds from the sky
the fur from the faces of
wild animals, crusts
from scabby eyes, scales from
the mind and husbands from wives

Lines on Receiving the Dial's Award: 1927

In the common mind, a corked bottle,
that senate's egg, today the prohibition
we all feel has been a little lifted

The sick carpenter fished up another bottle,
empty from his cellar
for me last week, an old ginflask—

What a beauty! a fat quartflask of
greenish glass, *The Father of His Country*
embossed upon the side of it
in glass letters capping the green profile
and on the other
A little more Grape Captain Bragg

A noteworthy antithesis, that, to petty
thievery on a large scale: generous
out of the sand, good to hold and to see—

It approaches poetry and my delight
at having been even for a moment shored
against a degradation
ticked off daily round me like the newspapers

An old, empty bottle in my hand
I go through the motions of drinking,
drinking to *The Dial* and its courtesy

The Red Lily

To the bob-white's call
and drone of reaper

tumbling daisies in the sun—
one by one

about the smutting panels of
white doors

grey shingles slip and fall—
But you, a loveliness

of even lines
curving to the throat, the

crossroads is your home.
You are, upon

your steady stem
one trumpeted wide flower

slightly tilted
above a scale of buds—

Sometimes a farmer's wife
gathers an armful

for her pitcher on the porch—
Topping a stone wall

against the shale-ledge
a field full—

By the road, the river
the edge of the woods

—opening in the sun
closing with the dark—

everywhere
Red Lily

in your common cup
all beauty lies—

Interests of 1926

It is spring
and we walk up the filthysweet
worn wooden stairs
to it, close by the miniature
bright poplar leaves
at a grimy window
wading . . . over the boards
of the second floor . . .
in the clear smile of
the boyish husband
all compassion for
her injury . . . . and
                    such is the
celebrated May

The Attic Which Is Desire

           the unused tent
           of

           bare beams
           beyond which

           directly wait
           the night

           and day—
           Here

           from the street
           by

               * * *
               * S *
               * O *
               * D *
               * A *
               * * *

           ringed with
           running lights

           the darkened
           pane

           exactly
           down the center
           is
           transfixed

This Is Just to Say

I have eaten
the plums
that were in
the icebox

and which
you were probably
saving
for breakfast

Forgive me
they were delicious
so sweet
and so cold

Birds and Flowers

I

It is summer, winter, any
time—
no time at all—but delight
the springing up
of those secret flowers
the others imitate and so

become round
extraordinary in petalage
yellow, blue

fluted and globed
slendercrimson
moonshaped—

in clusters on a wall.
                              Come!

And just now

you will not come, your
ankles
carry you another way, as

thought grown old—or
older—in
your eyes fire them against

me—small flowers
birds flitting here and there
between twigs

II

What have I done
to drive you away? It is
winter, true enough, but

this day I love you.
This day
there is no time at all

more than in under
my ribs where anatomists
say the heart is—

And just today you
will not have me. Well,
tomorrow it may be snowing—

I'll keep after you, your
repulse of me is no more
than a rebuff to the weather—

If we make a desert of
ourselves—we make
a desert . . .

III

Nothing is lost! the white
shellwhite
glassy, linenwhite, crystalwhite
crocuses with orange centers
the purple crocus with
an orange center, the yellow
crocus with a yellow center—

That which was large but
seemed spent of
power to fill the world with
its wave of splendor is
overflowing again into every
corner—

        Though the eye
turns inward, the mind
has spread its embrace—in
a wind that
roughs the stiff petals—
More! the particular flower is
blossoming . . .

An Elegy for D. H. Lawrence

An Elegy for D. H. Lawrence

Green points on the shrub
and poor Lawrence dead.
The night damp and misty
and Lawrence no more in the world
to answer April's promise
with a fury of labor
against waste, waste and life's
coldness.

Once he received a letter—
he never answered it—
praising him: so English
he had thereby raised himself
to an unenglish greatness.
Dead now and it grows clearer
what bitterness drove him.

This is the time.
The serpent in the grotto
water dripping from the stone
into a pool.
Mediterranean evenings. Ashes
of Cretan fires. And to the north
forsythia hung with
yellow bells in the cold.

Poor Lawrence
worn with a fury of sad labor
to create summer from
spring's decay. English
women. Men driven not to love
but to the ends of the earth.
The serpent turning his

stone-like head,
the fixed agate eyes turn also.

And unopened jonquils
hang their folded heads. No
summer. But for Lawrence
full praise in this
half cold half season—
before trees are in leaf and
tufted grass stars
unevenly the bare ground.

Slowly the serpent leans
to drink by the tinkling water
the forked tongue alert,
Then fold after fold,
glassy strength, passing
a given point,
as by desire drawn
forward bodily, he glides
smoothly in.

To stand by the sea or walk
again along a river's bank and talk
with a companion, to halt
watching where the edge of water
meets and lies upon
the unmoving shore—
Flood waters rise, and will rise,
rip the quiet valley
trap the gypsy and the girl
She clings drowning to
a bush in flower.

Remember, now, Lawrence dead.
Blue squills in bloom—to
the scorched aridity of

the Mexican plateau. Or baked
public squares in the cities of
Mediterranean islands
where one waits for busses and
boats come slowly along the water
arriving.

But the sweep of spring over
temperate lands, meadows and woods
where the young walk and talk
incompletely,
straining to no summer,
hearing the frogs, speaking of
birds and insects—

Febrile spring moves not to heat
but always more slowly,
burdened by a weight of leaves.
Nothing now
to burst the bounds—
remains confined by them. Heat,
heat! Unknown. Poor Lawrence,
dead and only the drowned
fallen dancing from the deck
of a pleasure boat
unfading desire.

Rabbits, imaginings, the
drama, literature, satire.
The serpent cannot move
his stony eyes, scarcely sees
but touching the air
with his forked tongue surmises
and his body which dipped
into the cold water
is gone.

Violently the satiric sun
that leads April not to
the panting dance but to stillness
in, into the brain, dips
and is gone also.
And sisters return
through the dusk
to the measured rancor
of their unbending elders.

Greep, greep, greep the cricket
chants where the snake
with agate eyes leaned to the water.
Sorrow to the young
that Lawrence has passed
unwanted from England.
And in the gardens forsythia
and in the woods
now the crinkled spice-bush
in flower.

Adam and Eve and the City

To a Wood Thrush

Singing across the orchard
before night, answered
from the depths
of the wood, inversely
and in a lower key—

First I tried to write
conventionally praising you
but found it no more
than my own thoughts
that I was giving. No.

What can I say?
           Vistas
of delight waking suddenly
before a cheated world.

Fine Work with Pitch and Copper

Now they are resting
in the fleckless light
separately in unison

like the sacks
of sifted stone stacked
regularly by twos

about the flat roof
ready after lunch
to be opened and strewn

The copper in eight
foot strips has been
beaten lengthwise

down the center at right
angles and lies ready
to edge the coping

One still chewing
picks up a copper strip
and runs his eye along it

Young Woman at a Window

She sits with
tears on

her cheek
her cheek on

her hand
the child

in her lap
his nose

pressed
to the glass

The Rose

First the warmth, variability
color and frailty

A grace of petals skirting
the tight-whorled cone

Come to generous abandon—
to the mind as to the eye

Wide! Wider!
Wide as if panting, until

the gold hawk's-eye speaks once
coldly its perfection

A Chinese Toy

Six whittled chickens
on a wooden bat

that peck within a
circle pulled

by strings fast to
a hanging weight

when shuttled by the
playful hand

La Belle Dame de Tous les Jours

It speaks, it moves
there is a sound and alteration—

The hair
about the brow, the eyes
symmetrically turn—

This has no part
in what has been but smiles
in selfishness
unique—

against the snow
new-fallen beyond
the tropic window-sill

Adam

He grew up by the sea
on a hot island
inhabited by negroes—mostly.
There he built himself
a boat and a separate room
close to the water
for a piano on which he practiced—
by sheer doggedness
and strength of purpose
striving
like an Englishman
to emulate his Spanish friend
and idol—the weather!

And there he learned
to play the flute—not very well—

Thence he was driven
out of Paradise—to taste
the death that duty brings
so daintily, so mincingly,
with such a noble air—
that enslaved him all his life
thereafter—

And he left behind
all the curious memories that come
with shells and hurricanes—
the smells
and sounds and glancing looks
that Latins know belong
to boredom and long torrid hours
and Englishmen

will never understand—whom
duty has marked
for special mention—with
a tropic of its own
and its own heavy-winged fowl
and flowers that vomit beauty
at midnight—

But the Latin has turned romance
to a purpose cold as ice.
He never sees
or seldom
what melted Adam's knees
to jelly and despair—and
held them up pontifically—

Underneath the whisperings
of tropic nights
there is a darker whispering
that death invents especially
for northern men
whom the tropics
have come to hold.

It would have been enough
to know that never,
never, never, never would
peace come as the sun comes
in the hot islands.
But there was
a special hell besides
where black women lie waiting
for a boy—

Naked on a raft
he could see the barracudas

waiting to castrate him
so the saying went—
Circumstances take longer—

But being an Englishman
though he had not lived in England
desde que avia cinco años
he never turned back
but kept a cold eye always
on the inevitable end
never wincing—never to unbend—
God's handyman
going quietly into hell's mouth
for a paper of reference—
fetching water to posterity
a British passport
always in his pocket—
muleback over Costa Rica
eating pâtés of black ants

And the Latin ladies admired him
and under their smiles
dartled the dagger of despair—
in spite of
a most thorough trial—
found his English heart safe
in the roseate steel. Duty
the angel
which with whip in hand . . .
—along the low wall of paradise
where they sat and smiled
and flipped their fans
at him—

He never had but the one home
Staring Him in the eye

coldly
and with patience—
without a murmur, silently
a desperate, unvarying silence
to the unhurried last.

Pardon my injuries
now that you are old—
Forgive me my awkwardnesses
my impatience
and short replies—
I sometimes detect in your face
a puzzled pity for me
your son—
I have never been close to you
—mostly your own fault;
in that I am like you.
It is as though
you looked down from above
at me—not
with what they would describe
as pride but the same
that is in me: a sort
of shame that the world
should see you as I see you,
a somewhat infantile creature—
without subtlety—
defenseless.

And because you are defenseless
I too, horribly,
take advantage of you,
(as you of me)
my mother, keep you
imprisoned—in
the name of protection
when you want so wildly to escape
as I wish also
to escape and leap into chaos

(where Time has
not yet begun)

When Adam died
it came out clearly—
Not what commonly
might have been supposed but
a demon, fighting for the fire
it needed to breathe
to live again.
A last chance. You
kicked blindly before you
and nearly broke your leg
against the metal—then sank
exhausted.
And that is the horror
of my guilt—and the sweetness
even at this late date
in some kind of acknowledgement

I realize why you wish
to communicate with the dead—
And it is again I
who try to hush you
that you shall not
make a fool of yourself
and have them stare at you
with natural faces—
Trembling, sobbing
and grabbing at the futile hands
till a mind goes sour
watching you—and flies off
sick at the mumbling
from which nothing clearly
is ever spoken—

It not so much frightens
as shames me. I want to protect
you, to spare you the disgrace—
seeing you reach out that way
to self-inflicted emptiness—

As if you were not able
to protect yourself—
and me too—if we did not
have to be so guarded—

Therefore I make this last plea:

Forgive me
I have been a fool—
(and remain a fool)
If you are not already too blind
too deaf, too lost in the past
to know or to care—
I will write a book about you—
making you live (in a book!)
as you still desperately
want to live—
to live always—unforgiving

I'll give you brandy
or wine
whenever I think you need it
(need it)
because it whips up
your mind and your senses
and brings color to your face
—to enkindle that life
too coarse for the usual,
that sly obscenity
that fertile darkness
in which passion mates—

reflecting
the lightnings of creation—
and the moon—
"C'est la vieillesse
inexorable qu'arrive!"

One would think
you would be reconciled with Time
instead of clawing at Him
that way, terrified
in the night—screaming out
unwilling, unappeased
and without shame—

Might He not take
that wasted carcass, crippled
and deformed, that ruined face
sightless, deafened—
the color gone—that seems
always listening, watching, waiting
ashamed only
of that single and last
degradation—
No. Never. Defenseless
still you would keep
every accoutrement
which He has loaned
till it shall be torn from
your grasp, a final grip
from those fingers
which cannot hold a knife
to cut the meat but which
in a hypnotic ecstasy
can so wrench a hand held out
to you that our bones
crack under the unwonted pressure—

St. Francis Einstein of the Daffodils

*On the first visit of Professor Einstein to
the United States in the spring of 1921.*

"Sweet land"
at last!
out of the sea—
the Venusremembering wavelets
rippling with laughter—
freedom
for the daffodils!
—in a tearing wind
that shakes
the tufted orchards—
Einstein, tall as a violet
in the lattice-arbor corner
is tall as
a blossomy peartree

A Samos, Samos
dead and buried. Lesbia
a black cat in the freshturned
garden. All dead.
All flesh they sung
is rotten
Sing of it no longer—

Side by side young and old
take the sun together—
maples, green and red
yellowbells
and the vermilion quinceflower
together—

The peartree
with fœtid blossoms
sways its high topbranches
with contrary motions
and there are both pinkflowered
and coralflowered peachtrees
in the bare chickenyard
of the old negro
with white hair who hides
poisoned fish-heads
here and there
where stray cats find them—
find them

Spring days
swift and mutable
winds blowing four ways
hot and cold
shaking the flowers—

Now the northeast wind
moving in fogs leaves the grass
cold and dripping. The night
is dark. But in the night
the southeast wind approaches.
The owner of the orchard
lies in bed
with open windows
and throws off his covers
one by one

The Death of See

One morning
the wind scouring
the streets

I read: Poet
and woman
found shot dead

Pact seen in
murder—
Suicide in

artist's suite—
Their bodies
fully clothed

were found
half covered
by

a blanket—
See
was described as

a poet
but when or
where his

poems were
published M. could
not say. . . .

Which adds
a certain
gravity—

Suddenly
snow trees
flashing

upon the mind
from a clean
world

To an Elder Poet

To be able
and not to do it

Still as a flower

No flame,
a flower spent
with heat—

lovely flower
            hanging
in the rain

                Never!

Soberly

Whiter than day

Wait forever
shaken by the rain
            forever

Perpetuum Mobile: The City

     —a dream
we dreamed
   each
separately
    we two

of love
   and of
desire—

that fused
in the night—

in the distance
   over
the meadows
   by day
impossible—
   The city
disappeared
   when
we arrived—

   A dream
a little false

toward which
   now
we stand
   and stare
transfixed—

All at once
        in the east
rising!

        All white!

        small
as a flower—

a locust cluster
a shad bush
        blossoming

Over the swamps
        a wild
magnolia bud—
        greenish
white
a northern
        flower—
And so
        we live
        looking—

At night
        it wakes
On the black
        sky—

a dream
        toward which
we love—
at night
        more
than a little
        false—

We have bred
we have dug
we have figured up
our costs
we have bought
an old rug—

We batter at our
unsatisfactory
          brilliance—

There is no end
          to desire—

Let us break
          through
and go there—

in
          vain!

—delectable
          amusement:

Milling about—

Money! in
armored trucks—
Two men
          walking
at two paces from
          each other
their right hands
          at the hip—
on the butt of
an automatic—

till they themselves
hold up the bank
and themselves
        drive off
for themselves
        the money
in an armored car—

        For love!

Carefully
        carefully tying
carefully

        selected
wisps of long
dark hair
        wisp
by wisp
upon the stubs
of his kinky wool—
For two hours
        they worked—
        until
he coiled
        the thick
knot upon
that whorish
        head—

Dragged
        insensible
upon his face
by the lines—

—a running horse

For love.

Their eyes
        blown out—

—for love, for love!

Neither the rain
Nor the storm—
can keep them

        for love!

from the daily
accomplishment
        of their
appointed rounds—

Guzzling
the creamy foods
        while
out of sight
        in
the sub-cellar—
the waste fat
the old vegetable
        chucked down
a chute
        the foulest
sink in the world—

And go
on the out-tide
ten thousands
        cots
floating to sea

                    like weed
that held back
the pristine ships—

And fattened there
an eel
in the water pipe—

            No end—

There!

            There!

There!

            —a dream
of lights
            hiding

the iron reason
            and stone
a settled
            cloud—

City

            whose stars
of matchless
            splendor—

            and
in bright-edged
            clouds
the moon—

                    bring

          silence

                    breathlessly—

          Tearful city
                    on a summer's day
          the hard grey
                    dwindling
          in a wall of
                    rain—

                    farewell!

Cancion

              (*Lupercio De Argensola*)

          Alivia sus fatigas
          El labrador cansado
          Quando su yerta barba escarcha cubre,
          Pensando en las espigas
          Del Agosto abrasado,
          Y en los lagares ricos del Octubre.

          The tired workman
          Takes his ease
          When his stiff beard's all frosted over
          Thinking of blazing
          August's corn
          And the brimming wine-cribs of October.

Morning

•

The Crimson Cyclamen

Morning

on the hill is cool! Even the dead
grass stems that start with the wind along
the crude board fence are less than harsh.

—a broken fringe of wooden and brick fronts
above the city, fading out,
beyond the watertank on stilts,
an isolated house or two here and there,
into the bare fields.

                           The sky is immensely
wide! No one about. The houses badly
numbered.

            Sun benches at the curb bespeak
another season, truncated poplars
that having served for shade
served also later for the fire. Rough
cobbles and abandoned car rails interrupted
by precipitous cross streets.

                        Down-hill
in the small, separate gardens (Keep out
you) bare fruit trees and among tangled
cords of unpruned grapevines low houses
showered by unobstructed light.

                       Pulley lines
to poles, on one a blue
and white tablecloth bellying easily.
Feather beds from windows and swathed in
old linoleum and burlap, fig trees. Barrels
over shrubs.

393

Level of

the hill, two old men walking and talking
come on together.

             —Firewood, all lengths
and qualities stacked behind patched
out-houses. Uses for ashes.
And a church spire sketched on the sky,
of sheet-metal and open beams, to resemble
a church spire—

               —These Wops are wise

                   —and walk about

absorbed among stray dogs and sparrows,
pigeons wheeling overhead, their
feces falling—

          or shawled and jug in hand
beside a concrete wall down which,
from a loose water-pipe, a stain descends,
the wall descending also, holding up
a garden—On its side the pattern of
the boards that made the forms is still
discernible. —to the oil-streaked
highway—

       Whence, turn and look where,
at the crest, the shoulders of a man
are disappearing gradually below the worn
fox-fur of tattered grasses—

               And round again, the
two old men in caps crossing at
a gutter now, *Pago, Pago!* still absorbed.

394

—a young man's face staring
from a dirty window—Women's Hats—and
at the door a cat, with one fore-foot on
the top step, looks back—

                              Scatubitch!

                    Sacks of flour
piled inside the bakery window, their
paley trade-marks flattened to
the glass—

          And with a stick,
scratching within the littered field—
old plaster, bits of brick—to find what
coming? In God's name! Washed out, worn
out, scavengered and rescavengered—

Spirit of place rise from these ashes
repeating secretly an obscure refrain:

This is my house and here I live.
Here I was born and this is my office—

—passionately leans examining, stirring
with the stick, a child following.
Roots, salads? Medicinal, stomachic?
Of what sort? Abortifacient? To be dug,
split, submitted to the sun, brewed
cooled in a teacup and applied?

                    Kid Hot
Jock, in red paint, smeared along
the fence.—and still remains, of—
if and if, as the sun rises, rolls and
comes again.

            But every day, every day
she goes and kneels—

                    died of tuberculosis
when he came back from the war, nobody
else in our family ever had it except a
baby once after that—

                        alone on the cold
floor beside the candled altar, stifled
weeping—and moans for his lost
departed soul the tears falling
and wiped away, turbid with her grime.

Covered, swaddled, pinched and saved
shrivelled, broken—to be rewetted and
used again.

The Crimson Cyclamen

(To the Memory of Charles Demuth)

White suffused with red
more rose than crimson
—all acolor
the petals flare back
from the stooping craters
of those flowers
as from a wind rising—
And though the light
that enfolds and pierces
them discovers blues
and yellows there also—
and crimson's a dull word
beside such play—
yet the effect against
this winter where
they stand—is crimson—

It is miraculous
that flower should rise
by flower
alike in loveliness—
as thought mirrors
of some perfection
could never be
too often shown—
silence holds them—
in that space. And
color has been construed
from emptiness
to waken there—

But the form came gradually.
The plant was there
before the flowers
as always—the leaves,
day by day changing. In
September when the first
pink pointed bud still
bowed below, all the leaves
heart-shaped
were already spread—
quirked and green
and stenciled with a paler
green
irregularly
across and round the edge—

Upon each leaf it is
a pattern more
of logic than a purpose
links each part to the rest,
an abstraction
playfully following
centripetal
devices, as of pure thought—
the edge tying by
convergent, crazy rays
with the center—
where that dips
cupping down to the
upright stem—the source
that has splayed out
fanwise and returns
upon itself in the design
thus decoratively—

Such are the leaves
freakish, of the air
as thought is, of roots
dark, complex from
subterranean revolutions
and rank odors
waiting for the moon—
The young leaves
coming among the rest
are more crisp
and deeply cupped
the edges rising first
impatient of the slower
stem—the older
level, the oldest
with the edge already
fallen a little backward—
the stem alone
holding the form
stiffly a while longer—

Under the leaf, the same
though the smooth green
is gone. Now the ribbed
design—if not
the purpose, is explained.
The stem's pink flanges,
strongly marked,
stand to the frail edge,
dividing, thinning
through the pink and downy
mesh—as the round stem
is pink also—cranking
to penciled lines
angularly deft

through all, to link together
the unnicked argument
to the last crinkled edge—
where the under and the over
meet and disappear
and the air alone begins
to go from them—
the conclusion left still
blunt, floating
if warped and quaintly flecked
whitened and streaked
resting
upon the tie of the stem—

But half hidden under them
such as they are
it begins that must
put thought to rest—

wakes in tinted beaks
still raising the head
and passion
is loosed—

its small lusts
addressed still to
the knees and to sleep—
abandoning argument

lifts
through the leaves
day by day
and one day opens!

The petals!
the petals undone

loosen all five and
swing up

The flower
flows to release—

Fast within a ring
where the compact
agencies
of conception

lie mathematically
ranged
round the
hair-like sting—

From such a pit
the color flows
over
a purple rim

upward to
the light! the light!
all around—
Five petals

as one
to flare, inverted
a full flower
each petal tortured

eccentrically
the while, warped edge
jostling
half-turned edge

side by side
until compact, tense
evenly stained
to the last fine edge

an ecstasy
from the empurpled ring
climbs up (though
firm there still)

each petal
by excess of tensions
in its own flesh
all rose—

rose red
standing until it
bends backward
upon the rest, above,

answering
ecstasy with excess
all together
acrobatically

not as if bound
(though still bound)
but upright
as if they hung

from above
to the streams
with which
they are veined and glow—
the frail fruit
by its frailty supreme

opening in the tense moment
to no bean
no completion
no root
no leaf and no stem
but color only and a form—

It is passion
earlier and later than thought
that rises above thought
at instant peril—peril
itself a flower
that lifts and draws it on—

Frailer than level thought
more convolute
rose red
highest
the soonest to wither
blacken
and fall upon itself
formless—

And the flowers
grow older and begin
to change, larger now
less tense, when at the full
relaxing, widening
the petals falling down
the color paling
through violaceous to
tinted white—

The structure of the petal
that was all red
beginning now to show

from a deep central vein
other finely scratched veins
dwindling to that edge
through which the light
more and more shows
fading through gradations
immeasurable to the eye—

The day rises and swifter
briefer
more frailly relaxed
than thought that still
holds good—the color
draws back while still
the flower grows
the rose of it nearly all lost
a darkness of dawning purple
paints a deeper afternoon—

The day passes
in a horizon of colors
all meeting
less severe in loveliness
the petals fallen now well back
till flower touches flower
all round
at the petal tips
merging into one flower—

Recent Verse 1938

Classic Scene

A power-house
in the shape of
a red brick chair
90 feet high

on the seat of which
sit the figures
of two metal
stacks—aluminum—

commanding an area
of squalid shacks
side by side—
from one of which

buff smoke
streams while under
a grey sky
the other remains

passive today—

Autumn

A stand of people
by an open

grave underneath
the heavy leaves

celebrates
the cut and fill

for the new road
where

an old man
on his knees

reaps a basket-
ful of

matted grasses for
his goats

The Term

A rumpled sheet
of brown paper
about the length

and apparent bulk
of a man was
rolling with the

wind slowly over
and over in
the street as

a car drove down
upon it and
crushed it to

the ground. Unlike
a man it rose
again rolling

with the wind over
and over to be as
it was before.

Weasel Snout

Staring she
kindles
the street windows

to daintiness—
Under
her driving looks

gems plainly
colored blue and
red and

green grow
fabulous again—She
is the modern marvel

the ray from
whose bulbous eyes
starts

through glass walls
to animate
dead things—

Advent of Today

South wind
striking in—torn
spume—trees

inverted over trees
scudding low
a sea become winged

bringing today
out of yesterday
in bursts of rain—

a darkened presence
above
detail of October grasses

veiled at once
in a downpour—
conflicting rattle of

the rain against
the storm's slow majesty—
leaves

rising
instead of falling
the sun

coming and going
toward the
middle parts of the sky

The Sun

lifts heavily
and cloud and sea
weigh upon the
unwaiting air—

Hasteless
the silence is
divided
by small waves

that wash away
night whose wave
is without
sound and gone—

Old categories
slacken
memoryless—
weed and shells where

in the night
a high tide left
its mark
and block of half

burned wood washed
clean—
The slovenly bearded
rocks hiss—

Obscene refuse
charms
this modern shore—
Listen!

it is a sea-snail
singing—
Relax, relent—
the sun has climbed

the sand is
drying—Lie
by the broken boat—
the eel-grass

bends
and is released
again—Go down, go
down past knowledge

shelly lace—
among the rot
of children
screaming

their delight—
logged
in the penetrable
nothingness

whose heavy body
opens
to their leaps
without a wound—

A Bastard Peace

        —where a heavy
woven-wire fence
topped with jagged ends, encloses
a long cinder-field by the river—

A concrete disposal tank at
one end, small wooden
pit-covers scattered about—above
sewer intakes, most probably—

Down the center's a service path
graced on one side by
a dandelion in bloom—and a white
butterfly—

The sun parches still
the parched grass. Along
the fence, blocked from the water
leans the washed-out street—

Three cracked houses—
a willow, two chickens, a
small boy, with a home-made push cart,
walking by, waving a whip—

Gid ap! No other traffic or
like to be.
There to rest, to improvise and
unbend! Through the fence

beyond the field and shining
water, 12 o'clock blows
but nobody goes
other than the kids from school—

The Poor

It's the anarchy of poverty
delights me, the old
yellow wooden house indented
among the new brick tenements

Or a cast-iron balcony
with panels showing oak branches
in full leaf. It fits
the dress of the children

reflecting every stage and
custom of necessity—
Chimneys, roofs, fences of
wood and metal in an unfenced

age and enclosing next to
nothing at all: the old man
in a sweater and soft black
hat who sweeps the sidewalk—

his own ten feet of it
in a wind that fitfully
turning his corner has
overwhelmed the entire city

To a Dead Journalist

Behind that white brow
now the mind simply sleeps—
the eyes, closed, the
lips, the mouth,

the chin, no longer useful,
the prow of the nose.
But rumors of the news,
unrealizable,

cling still among those
silent, butted features, a
sort of wonder at
this scoop

come now, too late:
beneath the lucid ripples
to have found so monstrous
an obscurity.

Africa

Quit writing
and in Morocco
raise a beard

Go without a hat
like poor Clew
who braved

the desert heat.
Or if you will
like Herb

sit on a hotel
balcony and
watch your ship

while the girls
bring wines
and food

to you privately.
The language?
Make money.

Organize
The language.
Right.

Lovely Ad

All her charms
are bubbles
from a tilted
cigarette—

And look!
she sees
to light them
his face!

Whereas for us
his sleek
black hair
is hint enough.

4th of July

I

The ship moves
but its smoke
moves with the wind
faster than the ship

—thick coils of it
through leafy trees
pressing
upon the river

II

The heat makes
this place of the woods
a room
in which two robins pain

crying
distractedly
over the plight of
their unhappy young

III

During the explosions
at dawn, the celebrations
I could hear
a native cuckoo

in the distance
as at dusk, before
I'd heard
a night hawk calling

The Defective Record

Cut the bank for the fill.
Dump sand
pumped out of the river
into the old swale

killing whatever was
there before—including
even the muskrats. Who did it?
There's the guy.

Him in the blue shirt and
turquoise skullcap.
Level it down
for him to build a house

on to build a
house on to build a house on
to build a house
on to build a house on to . . .

Middle

of this profusion
a robin flies carrying
food on its tongue
and a flag

red white and
blue hangs
motionless. Return
from the sick

wean the mind
again from among
the foliage also of
infection. There

is a brass band at
the monument
and the children
that paraded

the blistering streets
are giving lustily
to the memory
of our war dead.

A Fond Farewell

You? Why you're
just sucking
my life blood out.

What do I care
if the baker
and the garbage man

must be served.
Take what
you might give

and be damned
to you. I'm
going elsewhere.

The Unknown

Do you exist
my pretty bird
flying
above the snow?

Are you actually
flying
or do I imagine
it so?

Detail of wing
and breast
unquestionably
there—

Or do I merely
think you
perfect
in mid-air?

CODA

Beating heart
feather
of wing and breast

to this
bleakness
antithetical

In love
dear love, my love
detail is all

Porous

Cattail fluff
blows in
at the bank door,

and on wings
of chance
the money floats out,

lighter than a dream,
through the heavy walls
and vanishes.

The Petunia

Purple!
for months unknown
but for
the barren sky.

A purple trumpet
fragile
as our hopes
from the very
sand
saluting us.

The Graceful Bastion

A white butterfly
in an August garden,
light as it may seem

among the zinnias
and verbenas,
fragile among the red

trumpeted petunias,
is ribbed with steel
wired to the sun

whose triumphant power
will keep it safe,
free as laughter,

secure against
bombardments no more
dangerous to its

armored might than if
the cotton clouds
should merely fall.

The Return to Work

Promenading their
skirted galleons of sex,
the two office assistants

rock unevenly
together
down the broad stairs,

one
(as I follow slowly
in the trade wind

of my admiration)
gently
slapping her thighs.

The Deceptrices

Because they are not,
they paint their lips
and dress like whores.

Because they are uncertain,
they put on the bold
looks of experience.

This is their youth, too
soon gone, too soon
the unalterable conclusion.

Detail

Her milk don't seem to ..
She's always hungry but ..
She seems to *gain* all right,
I don't know.

Detail

Doc, I bin lookin' for you
I owe you two bucks.

How you doin'?

Fine. When I get it
I'll bring it up to you.

Detail

Hey!
Can I have some more
milk?

YEEEEAAAAASSSSS!
—always the gentle
mother!

Detail

I had a misfortune in September,
just at the end of my vacation.

I been keepin' away from that for years.
Just an accident. No foundation.

None at all, no feeling. I'm too
old to have a child. Why I'm fifty!

Their Most Prized Possession—

        their liberty—
                Hands behind a coat
shiny green. Tall, the eyes
downcast—
            Sunlight through a clutter of
wet clouds, lush weeds—
                  The oriole!
Hungry as an oriole.

Unnamed

From "Paterson"

1

Your lovely hands
Your lovely tender hands!
Reflections of what grace
what heavenly joy

predicted for the world
in knowing you—
blest, as am I, and humbled
by such ecstasy.

2

When I saw
the flowers

I was
thunderstruck!

You should not
have been—

Tulips, she said
and smiled.

3

I bought a new
bathing suit

Just pants
and a brassiere—

I haven't shown
it

to my mother
yet.

4

Better than flowers
is a view of yourself
my darling—

I'm so glad you came
I thought I should never
see you again.

At the Bar

Hi, open up a dozen.

Wha'cha tryin' ta do—
charge ya batteries?

Make it two.

Easy girl!
You'll blow a fuse if
ya keep that up.

Graph for Action

Don't say "humbly".
"Respectfully", yes
but not "humbly".

And the Committee
both farted
and that settled it.

Breakfast

> Twenty sparrows
> on
>
> a scattered
> turd:
>
> Share and share
> alike.

To Greet a Letter-Carrier

> Why'n't you bring me
> a good letter? One with
> lots of money in it.
> I could make use of that.
> Atta boy! Atta boy!

These

are the desolate, dark weeks
when nature in its barrenness
equals the stupidity of man.

The year plunges into night
and the heart plunges
lower than night

to an empty, windswept place
without sun, stars or moon
but a peculiar light as of thought

that spins a dark fire—
whirling upon itself until,
in the cold, it kindles

to make a man aware of nothing
that he knows, not loneliness
itself—Not a ghost but

would be embraced—emptiness,
despair—(They
whine and whistle) among

the flashes and booms of war;
houses of whose rooms
the cold is greater than can be thought,

the people gone that we loved,
the beds lying empty, the couches
damp, the chairs unused—

433

Hide it away somewhere
out of the mind, let it get roots
and grow, unrelated to jealous

ears and eyes—for itself.
In this mine they come to dig—all.
Is this the counterfoil to sweetest

music? The source of poetry that
seeing the clock stopped, says,
The clock has stopped

that ticked yesterday so well?
and hears the sound of lakewater
splashing—that is now stone.

The Drunkard

The Drunkard

(This poem, recently recovered, was sent by me to my mother in the fall of 1923 accompanied by a letter in part as follows:

Dearest Mother: Here is a poem to set beside some of my "incomprehensible" latter work. I think you will like this one. It seems the sort of thing that I am going to do. Art is a curious command. We must do what we are bidden to do and can go only so far as the light permits. I am always earnest as you, if anyone, must know. But no doubt I puzzle you—as I do myself. Plenty of love from your son. W.)

You drunken
tottering
bum

by Christ
in spite of all
your filth

and sordidness
I envy
you

It is the very face
of love
itself

abandoned
in that powerless
committal

to despair

Paterson: Episode 17

Beat hell out of it
   Beautiful Thing
   spotless cap
and crossed white straps
over the dark rippled cloth—
   Lift the stick
above that easy head
where you sit by the ivied
church, one arm
   buttressing you
long fingers spread out
among the clear grass prongs—
   and drive it down
   Beautiful Thing
that your caressing body kiss
   and kiss again
that holy lawn—

And again: obliquely—
legs curled under you as a
   deer's leaping—
pose of supreme indifference
   sacrament
to a summer's day
   Beautiful Thing
in the unearned suburbs
   then pause
   the arm fallen—
what memories
of what forgotten face
brooding upon that lily stem?

          The incredible
nose straight from the brow
    the empurpled lips
and dazzled half-sleepy eyes
    Beautiful Thing
of some trusting animal
    makes a temple
of its place of savage slaughter
    revealing
the damaged will incites still
    to violence
consummately beautiful thing
and falls about your resting
    shoulders—

Gently! Gently!
as in all things an opposite
    that awakes
the fury, conceiving
    knowledge
by way of despair that has
    no place
to lay its glossy head—
Save only—Not alone!
    Never, if possible
alone! to escape the accepted
    chopping block
and a square hat!—

And as reverie gains and
    your joints loosen
    the trick's done!
Day is covered and we see you—
    but not alone!
drunk and bedraggled to release
the strictness of beauty

under a sky full of stars
   Beautiful Thing
and a slow moon—
                              The car
   had stopped long since
   when the others
came and dragged those out
   who had you there
   indifferent
to whatever the anesthetic
   Beautiful Thing
might slum away the bars—
Reek of it!
   What does it matter?
   could set free
only the one thing—
But you!
—in your white lace dress
   "the dying swan"
and high heeled slippers—tall
as you already were—
   till your head
through fruitful exaggeration
was reaching the sky and the
prickles of its ecstasy
   Beautiful Thing!

And the guys from Paterson
   beat up
the guys from Newark and told
them to stay the hell out
of their territory and then
socked you one
   across the nose
   Beautiful Thing
for good luck and emphasis

cracking it
till I must believe that all
desired women have had each
    in the end
    a busted nose
and live afterward marked up
    Beautiful Thing
    for memory's sake
to be credible in their deeds

Then back to the party!
    and they maled
and femaled you jealously
    Beautiful Thing
as if to discover when and
    by what miracle
there should escape what?
still to be possessed
out of what part
    Beautiful Thing
should it look?
    or be extinguished—
Three days in the same dress
    up and down—
    It would take
a Dominie to be patient
    Beautiful Thing
with you—

The stroke begins again—
    regularly
automatic
    contrapuntal to
the flogging
like the beat of famous lines
in the few excellent poems

woven to make you
    gracious
and on frequent occasions
    foul drunk
    Beautiful Thing
pulse of release
    to the attentive
and obedient mind.

The Last Words of My English Grandmother

1920

There were some dirty plates
and a glass of milk
beside her on a small table
near the rank, disheveled bed—

Wrinkled and nearly blind
she lay and snored
rousing with anger in her tones
to cry for food,

Gimme something to eat—
They're starving me—
I'm all right I won't go
to the hospital. No, no, no

Give me something to eat
Let me take you
to the hospital, I said
and after you are well

you can do as you please.
She smiled, Yes
you do what you please first
then I can do what I please—

Oh, oh, oh! she cried
as the ambulance men lifted
her to the stretcher—
Is this what you call

making me comfortable?
By now her mind was clear—
Oh you think you're smart
you young people,

she said, but I'll tell you
you don't know anything.
Then we started.
On the way

we passed a long row
of elms. She looked at them
awhile out of
the ambulance window and said,

What are all those
fuzzy-looking things out there?
Trees? Well, I'm tired
of them and rolled her head away.

The Waitress

No wit (and none needed) but
the silence of her ways, grey eyes in
a depth of black lashes—
The eyes look and the look falls.

There is no way, no way. So close
one may feel the warmth of the cheek and yet
            there is
no way.

The benefits of poverty are a roughened skin
of the hands, the broken
knuckles, the stained wrists.

            Serious. Not as the others.
All the rest are liars, all but you.
                        Wait on us.
Wait on us, the hair held back practically
by a net, close behind the ears, at the sides of
the head. But the eyes—
                  but the mouth, lightly (quickly)
touched with rouge.
The black dress makes the hair dark, strangely
enough, and the white dress makes it light.
There is a mole under the jaw, low under
the right ear—
            And what arms!
                  The glassruby ring
on the fourth finger of the left hand.
                  —and the movements
under the scant dress as the weight of the tray
makes the hips shift forward slightly in lifting
and beginning to walk—

The Nominating Committee presents the following
resolutions, etc. etc. etc. All those
in favor signify by saying, Aye. Contrariminded,
No.
   Carried.
            And aye, and aye, and aye!

And the way the bell-hop runs downstairs:
      ta tuck a
         ta tuck a
            ta tuck a
               ta tuck a
                  ta tuck a
and the gulls in the open window screaming over
      the slow
break of the cold waves—

         O unlit candle with the soft white
plume, Sunbeam Finest Safety Matches all together in
a little box—

         And the reflections of both in
the mirror and the reflection of the hand, writing
writing—
         Speak to me of her!

         —and nobody else and nothing else
in the whole city, not an electric sign of shifting
colors, fourfoot daisies and acanthus fronds going
               from
red to orange, green to blue—forty feet across—

               Wait on us, wait
on us with your momentary beauty to be enjoyed by
none of us. Neither by you, certainly,
                  nor by me.

A Marriage Ritual

                                        Above
the darkness of a river upon
winter's icy sky
dreams the silhouette of the city:

This is my own! a flower,
a fruit, an animal by itself—

It does not recognize me
and never will. Still, it is my own
and my heart goes out to it
dumbly—

        but eloquently in
my own breast for you whom I love
—and cannot express what
my love is, how it varies, though
I waste it—

        It is
a river flowing through refuse
the dried sticks of weeds
and falling shell-ice lilac
from above as if with thoughts
of you—

This is my face and its moods
my moods, a riffled whiteness
shaken by the flow
that's constant in its swiftness
as a pool—

A Polack in
the stinging wind, her arms
wrapped to her breast
comes shambling near. To look
at what? downstream. It is
an old-world flavor: the poor
the unthrifty, passionately biased
by what errors of conviction—

Now a boy
is rolling a stout metal drum
up from below the river bank.
The woman and the boy, two
thievish figures, struggle with
the object. . . . in this light!

And still
there is one leafless tree
just at the water's edge and—

my face
constant to you!

The Swaggering Gait

Bareheaded
the hair blond in tight curls
the heavy and worn

blue sweater
buttoned tight
under a cold sky

he walks
and lifts the butt of cigar
he holds

to his pursing lips
alone—
save for the tilt

of his shoulders
the swing of his knees—
Even the paper

lunch bag in his other hand
sharing
that one distinction

The Predicter of Famine

White day, black river
corrugated and swift—

as the stone of the sky
on the prongy ring
of the tarnished city
is smooth and without motion:

A gull flies low
upstream, his beak tilted
sharply, his eye
alert to the providing water.

Illegitimate Things

Water still flows—
The thrush still sings

though in
the skirts of the sky

at the bottom of
the distance

huddle
. . . . echoing cannon!

Whose silence revives
valley after

valley to peace
as poems still conserve

the language
of old ecstasies.

The Province

The figure
of tall
white grass
by the cinder-bank
keeps its alignment
faultlessly.
Moves!
in the brilliant
channels
of the wind

Shines!
its polished
shafts
and feathered
fronds
ensconced there
colorless
beyond all feeling

This is
the principle
of the godly,
fluted, a
statue
tall and pale
—lifeless
save only in
beauty,
the kernel
of all seeking,
the eternal

The Brilliance

Oh sock, sock, sock!
brief but persistent.
Emulate the gnat
or a tree's leaves

that are not the tree
but mass to shape it.
Finis! Finish
and get out of this.

Fragment

My God, Bill, what have you done?

What do you think I've done? I've
opened up the world.

Where did you get them? Marvellous
beautiful!

Where does all snot come from? Under
the nose,

Yea-uh?

—the gutter, where everything comes
from, the manure heap.

The Yellow Season

The black, long-tailed,
one then, unexpectedly, another
glide easily on a curtain
of yellow leaves, upward—

The season wakens! loveliness
chirping and barking stands
among the branches, its
narrow-clawed toes and furry
hands moving in the leaves—

Round white eyes dotted with
jet live still, alert—in
all gentleness! unabated
beyond the cackle
of death's stinking certainty.

Mistrust of the Beloved

At the height of love
a darkness intervenes:
I hated you the whole
first year.

It will reawaken.
Be patient. (Ah but what
of the need to be
patient?)

It will reawaken by
somersaults
and see-saws, your hatred
will reawaken.

Passer Domesticus

Mistrust of the Beloved

Shabby little bird
I suppose it's
the story every-
where, if you're

domestic you're drab.
Peep peep!
the nightingale
's your cousin but

these flagrant
amours get you no-
where. Dull
to the eye you have

crept in unmolested.

The United States

The government of your body, sweet,
shall be my model for the world.
There is no desire in me to rule
that world or to advise it. Look
how it rouses with the sun, shuts
with night and sleeps fringed by
the slowly turning stars. I boil
I freeze before its tropics and its
cold. Its shocks are mine and to
the peaceful legislature of its seas,
by you its president,
I yield my willing services.

The Sun Bathers

A tramp thawing out
on a doorstep
against an east wall
Nov. 1, 1933:

a young man begrimed
and in an old
army coat
wriggling and scratching

while a fat negress
in a yellow-house window
nearby
leans out and yawns

into the fine weather

Sparrow Among Dry Leaves

The sparrows
by the iron fence-post
hardly seen

for the dry leaves
that half
cover them—

stirring up
the leaves—fight
and chirp

stridently
search
and

peck the sharp
gravel to
good digestion

and love's
obscure and insatiable
appetite

The Men

Wherein is Moscow's dignity
more than Passaic's dignity?
A few men have added color better
to the canvas, that's all.

The river is the same
the bridges are the same
there is the same to be discovered
of the sun—

Look how cold, steelgrey
run the waters of the Passaic.
The Church-of-the-Polaks'
bulbous towers

kiss the sky just so sternly
so dreamily
as in Warsaw, as in Moscow—
Violet smoke rises

from the mill chimneys—Only
the men are different who see it
draw it down in their minds
or might be different

Song

The black-winged gull
of love is flying—
hurl of the waters'
futile might!

Tirelessly
his deft strokes plying
he skims free in the licking
waves' despite—

There is no lying
to his shrill mockery
of their torment
day or night.

Descent

From disorder (a chaos)
order grows
—grows fruitful.
The chaos feeds it. Chaos
feeds the tree.

You Have Pissed Your Life

Any way you walk
Any way you turn
Any way you stand
Any way you lie
You have pissed your life

From an ineffectual fool
butting his head blindly
against obstacles, become
brilliant—focusing,
performing accurately to
a given end—

Any way you walk
Any way you turn
Any way you stand
Any way you lie
You have pissed your life

Moon and Stars

January! The beginning!
A moon
scoured by the wind
calls

from its cavern. A vacant
eye
stares. The wind
howls.

Among bones in rose flesh
singing
wake the stormy
stars.

The Girl

The wall, as I watched, came neck-high
to her walking difficultly
seaward of it over sand and stones. She

made the effort, mounted it while I
had my head turned, I merely
saw her on top at the finish rolling

over. She stood up dusted off her skirt
then there lifted her feet
unencumbered to skip dancing away

Simplex Sigilum Veri

an american papermatch packet
closed, gilt with a panel insert,
the bank, a narrow building
black, in a blue sky, puffs of

white cloud, the small windows
in perspective, bright green grass—
a sixinch metal tray, polished
bronze, holding a blue pencil

hexagonal, its bright brassy
butt catching the window light,
the dullred eraser half worn
down and a cheap brownenameled

pen-holder rest on the brown
marbled field of the stained blotter
by an oystershell smudged
with cigarette ash, a primrose plant

in a gold-ringed saucer, flowerless—
surfaces of all sorts
bearing printed characters, bottles
words printed on the backs of

two telephone directories, titles
for poems, The Advertising Biographical
Calendar of Medicine, Wednesday 18
Thursday 19, Friday 20, papers

of various shades sticking out
from under others, throwing

463

the printing out of line: portrait
of all that which we have lost,

a truncated pyramid, bronzed
metal (probably the surface
only) to match the tray, to which
a square, hinged lid is fixed,

the inkstand, from whose
imagined top the Prince of Wales
having climbed up, once with all
his might drove a golf ball.

The Phoenix and the Tortoise

The link between Barnum and Calas
is the freak
against which Rexroth rages,
the six-legged cow, the legless woman

for each presents a social concept
seeking approval, a pioneer society
and a modern asserting the norm
by stress of the Minotaur.

It's a legitimate manoeuvre,
perhaps it is all art
and Barnum our one genius (in the arts)
on the moral plane: the freak

and the athlete: the circus,
by which we return from Agamemnon
sober to our tasks—of pleasure—
and to our minds. If so,

in spite of Rexroth, Barnum
our Aeschylus, we
should show ourselves
more courteous to Calas the Greek

who has come from Oxford via Paris
to enlighten us, affect
less flippancy toward his
Confound the Wise:

"If, in a study such as this, in which the ideas of the
writer are discussed, we stop short at questions concerning
form, it is because forms—and I hope this appears clearly

465

in everything I have so far said—are for us tightly bound up with ideas and feelings. On this point I am a monist and opposed to the positivistic and dualistic habits that the last century has bequeathed us. Any error concerning form is consequently a fundamental error, and when ideas are erroneous and when feelings are untrue, then conformity bursts out and appears in form."

                              Read of Miranda

> the Portuguese torso—connoting
> Rexroth's Tortoise, say what he will:
> read one then the other,
> moral concepts both, curiously linked,
>
> by which in time we may
> behold, "the sun set where it did arise
> and moons grow into virgins' eyes,
> post sprout leaves and turn a tree and
>
> morbid fruit normality," as in
> the fluctuating molecule; details of
> The Greatest Show on Earth—if
> the mind survive and I be an American.

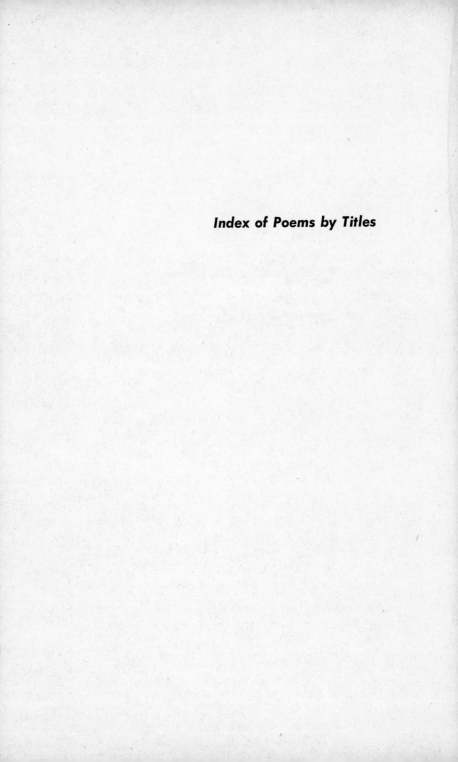

Index of Poems by Titles

Index of Poems by Titles

A Bastard Peace 414

A Celebration 188

A Chinese Toy 370

A Coronal 38

A Fond Farewell 422

A Good Night 192

A Marriage Ritual 447

A Poem for Norman MacLeod 114

A Portrait in Greys 160

A Portrait of the Times 92

A Prelude 141

Adam 371

Ad Infinitum 28

Advent of Today 411

Africa 417

All the Fancy Things 321

An After Song 22

An Early Martyr 85

An Elegy for D. H. Lawrence 361

Apology 131

Appeal 24

Approach of Winter 197

469

April   190

Arrival   215

At Night   191

At the Ball Game   284

At the Bar   431

At the Faucet of June   251

Autumn   408

Ballet   169

Berket and the Stars   191

Between Walls   343

Birds and Flowers   355

Blizzard   198

Blueflags   225

Breakfast   432

Brilliant Sad Sun   324

Cancion   390

Canthara   143

Chicory and Daisies   122

Classic Scene   407

Complaint   199

Complete Destruction   207

Composition   260

470

Con Brio   31
Conquest   172
Contemporania   29
Crude Lament   22

Daisy   208
Danse Russe   148
Dawn   138
Death   78
Death the Barber   264
Dedication for a Plot of Ground   171
Della Primavera Trasportata Al Morale   57
Descent   460
Detail   427
Detail   428
Drink   140

El Hombre   140
Epitaph   212
Eve   375

Fine Work with Pitch and Copper   368
Fire Spirit   24
First Praise   17
                                                    471

First Version: 1915   173
Fish   177
Flight to the City   244
Flowers by the Sea   87
4th of July   419
Fragment   453
From "The Birth of Venus," Song   20
Full Moon   65

Good Night   145
Graph for Action   431
Great Mullen   211
Gulls   126

Hemmed-in Males   322
Hero   139
Hic Jacet   30
History   49
Homage   18
Horned Purple   273
Hymn to Love Ended   108

Illegitimate Things   451
Immortal   21

472

Impromptu: The Suckers   315
In Harbor   128
In the 'Sconset Bus   338
Interests of 1926   352
Invocation and Conclusion   105
Item   95
It Is a Living Coral   325

January   197
January Morning   162

K. McB.   157
Keller Gegen Dom   147

La Belle Dame de Tous les Jours   370
Late for Summer Weather   100
Le Médecin Malgré Lui   36
Libertad! Igualidad! Fraternidad!   134
Light Becomes Darkness   266
Lighthearted William   226
Lines   206
Lines on Receiving the Dial's Award: 1927   350
Love Song   125
Love Song   137
                                                    473

Love Song   174
Lovely Ad   418
Man in a Room   37
March   43
M. B.   144
Memory of April   207
Metric Figure   123
Mezzo Forte   21
Middle   421
Mistrust of the Beloved   455
Moon and Stars   462
Morning   393
Mujer   149

Nantucket   348
New England   335

On Gay Wallpaper   345
Overture to a Dance of Locomotives   194

Passer Domesticus   456
Pastoral   121
Pastoral   124
Pastoral   161

474

Paterson   233
Paterson: Episode 17   438
Peace on Earth   15
Perpetuum Mobile: The City   384
Play   206
Poem   340
Porous   424
Portent   27
Portrait of a Lady   40
Portrait of a Woman in Bed   150
Portrait of the Author   228
Postlude   16
Primrose   209
Proletarian Portrait   101
Promenade   132

Queen-Ann's-Lace   210
Quietness   277

Rain   74
Rapid Transit   282
Rigamarole   278
Riposte   156
Romance Moderne   181
                                        475

Sea-Trout and Butterfish   91

Shoot it Jimmy!   269

Sicilian Emigrant's Song   35

Simplex Sigilum Veri   463

Sluggishly   341

Smell!   153

Song   460

Sparrow Among Dry Leaves   458

Spouts   222

Spring   205

Spring and All   241

Spring Song   119

Spring Storm   202

Spring Strains   159

St. Francis Einstein of the Daffodils   379

Struggle of Wings   291

Sub Terra   117

Summer Song   135

Sunday   109

Sympathetic Portrait of a Child   155

The Agonized Spires   262

The Attic Which Is Desire   353

The Avenue of Poplars   280

The Birds   218

The Bird's Companion   69

The Black Winds   245

The Botticellian Trees   80

The Brilliance   453

The Bull   336

The Catholic Bells   111

The Cod Head   333

The Cold Night   203

The Crimson Cyclamen   397

The Dark Day   201

The Dead Baby   113

The Death of Franco of Cologne: His Prophecy of
   Beethoven   25

The Death of See   381

The Deceptrices   426

The Defective Record   420

The Descent of Winter   297

The Desolate Field   196

The Disputants   218

The Drunkard   437

The Eyeglasses   256

The Farmer   243

The Flower   236

477

The Flowers Alone   90

The Fool's Song   19

The Gentle Man   205

The Girl   462

The Graceful Bastion   425

The Great Figure   230

The Hermaphroditic Telephones   286

The House   70

The Hunter   214

The Jungle   342

The Last Words of My English Grandmother   443

The Late Singer   187

The Lily   344

The Locust Tree in Flower   93

The Locust Tree in Flower   94

The Lonely Street   227

The Men   459

The Nightingales   224

The Ogre   154

The Old Men   158

The Ordeal   23

The Petunia   424

The Phoenix and the Tortoise   465

The Poor   206

478

The Poor   415
The Pot of Flowers   242
The Predicter of Famine   450
The Province   452
The Raper from Passenack   103
The Red Lily   351
The Red Wheelbarrow   277
The Return to Work   426
The Revelation   39
The Right of Way   258
The Rose   249
The Rose   369
The Sea   275
The Sea-Elephant   71
The Shadow   120
The Soughing Wind   205
The Source   346
The Sun   412
The Sun Bathers   457
The Swaggering Gait   449
The Term   409
The Thinker   220
The Tulip Bed   221
The Trees   66
                                    479

The Unknown   423

The United States   457

The Waitress   445

The Wanderer   3

The Widow's Lament in Springtime   223

The Wildflower   287

The Wind Increases   68

The Winds   349

The Yachts   106

The Yellow Season   454

The Young Housewife   136

The Young Laundryman   204

Their Most Prized Possession—   428

These   433

This Florida: 1924   329

This Is Just to Say   354

Thursday   202

Time the Hangman   204

To a Dead Journalist   416

To a Friend   205

To a Friend Concerning Several Ladies   216

To a Mexican Pig-Bank   98

To a Poor Old Woman   99

To a Solitary Disciple   167

480

To a Wood Thrush 367

To an Elder Poet 383

To an Old Jaundiced Woman 268

To Be Closely Written On A Small Piece of Paper 203

To Elsie 270

To Greet a Letter-Carrier 432

To Have Done Nothing 247

To Mark Anthony in Heaven 33

To Waken An Old Lady 200

To Wish Myself Courage 32

Tract 129

Transitional 34

Tree and Sky 102

Trees 142

Unnamed 429

View of a Lake 96

Virtue 152

Waiting 213

Weasel Snout 410

Wild Orchard 88

481

Willow Poem   196
Winter   89
Winter Quiet   141
Winter Sunset   127
Winter Trees   201

You Have Pissed Your Life   461
Young Love   253
Young Sycamore   332
Young Woman at a Window   369
Youth and Beauty   219